Dis

Trademarks

Contents

Your feedback is invaluable to us

If you recently bought this book, we would love to hear from you!

You can do this by writing a review on Amazon (or the online store where you purchased this book) about your last purchase! As part of our continual service improvement process, we love to hear real client experiences and feedback.

How does it work?

To post a review on Amazon, just log in to your account and click on the Create Your Own Review button (under Customer Reviews) of the relevant product page. You can find examples of product reviews in Amazon. If you purchased from another online store, simply follow their procedures.

Program Manager

Program Manager 2651 Self Assessment & Interview Preparation Questions:

Scheduling

1. How did you assign priorities to Program Manager jobs?

2. How did you go about making Program Manager job assignments?

3. Describe the most difficult scheduling Program Manager problem you have faced

4. When all have been over-loaded, how do your people meet Program Manager job assignments?

Behavior

1. Tell me about a time when you faced frustration. How did you deal with it?

2. Did you ever not meet your Program Manager goals?

3. What Are Your Program Manager Goals?

4. How often do other Program Manager staff treat you the way you want them to?

5. What s the last, best Program Manager business book you have read and what did you learn or applied that learning?

6. What else could you do to calm an angry Program Manager customer?

7. What did you like most about your last Program Manager job?

8. Tell me about a time when you had to give someone difficult Program Manager feedback. How did you handle it?

9. Have you ever started something up from nothing – give an Program Manager example?

10. Can you do this?

11. What would you do if an angry 4-H client came in the door?

12. How do you handle working with people who annoy

you?

13. Describe a recent Program Manager problem in which you included your subordinates in arriving at a solution?

14. How have you broken the ice in a first conversation with a Program Manager customer?

15. What is your Program Manager idea of the perfect job?

16. To what extent did a project test your comprehension Program Manager skills and technical knowledge?

17. Are you comfortable about working on many Program Manager projects at once?

18. How do you rate yourself in Program Manager terms of creativity in the fields of art, writing, and music?

19. What are some of the books youve read recently?

20. Tell me about your current top priorities. How did you determine that they should be your top priorities?

21. What have you done to remotivate a demoralized Program Manager team/person?

22. Describe some times when you were not very satisfied or pleased with your Program Manager performance. What did you do about it?

23. If you could relive your Program Manager college experiences, what would you do differently?

24. Can you tell us about a Program Manager situation where you found it challenging to build a trusting relationship with another individual?

25. How long did you serve?

26. How did you decide on your major?

27. How do you ensure others repeat positive behavior?

28. Can you tell us about a really difficult Program Manager decision you had to make at work recently?

29. Describe the most difficult Program Manager team you worked on, what was your role, and what knowledge have you applied?

30. Why are you better suited for this position than other Program Manager candidates?

31. Whats your nationality?

32. What are your Program Manager strengths, weaknesses, interests and career goals?

33. Have you had to convince a Program Manager team to work on a project they werent thrilled about?

34. What is your name?

35. When were you born?

36. What has been your most significant work related disappointment?

37. What achievements from your past work experience are you most proud of?

38. What Program Manager things did you fail to do?

39. When do you feel you have had to make personal sacrifices in order to get the Program Manager job done?

40. How will you get to work?

41. What was the most complex assignment you have had?

42. Describe a Program Manager problem you worked on as a team member ?

43. What processes have you used to build a Program Manager team?

44. Have you ever had your wages garnished?

45. What Program Manager kind of a project/task/ assignment wouldnt you delegate?

46. What would be the best Program Manager example of your ability to be flexible and adaptable?

47. Whats your typical approach to conflict?

48. What are you personally looking for in a successful Program Manager candidate?

49. When has it been necessary for you to tolerate an ambiguous Program Manager situation at work?

50. How can you start preparing now?

51. Take us through a complicated project you were responsible for planning. How did you define and measure Program Manager success?

52. Do you have children at home?

53. How did you know established methods wouldnt work?

54. What do you see yourself doing in ten Program Manager years?

55. Did you every make a risky Program Manager decision?

56. Tell me about a time you had to handle multiple responsibilities. How did you organize the work you needed to do?

57. Could you share with us recent Program Manager accomplishment of which you were particularly proud?

58. What are the most common forms of political behavior that you see in your work Program Manager environment?

59. What Program Manager kind of influencing techniques did you use?

60. Have you ever been on a Program Manager team where someone was not pulling their own weight? How did you handle it?

61. Are you for or against unions?

62. How did you organize the work you needed to do?

63. Tell me about a time where you had to deal with conflict on the Program Manager job.

64. In your position as _____, how did you determine which duties to Program Manager delegate to subordinates?

65. Can you tell me about a Program Manager job experience in which you had to speak up and tell other people what you thought or felt?

66. Sometimes it is necessary to work in unsettled or rapidly changing circumstances. When have you found yourself in this position?

67. Aside from your formal academic Program Manager education, can you think of something you have done to grow professionally in the recent past?

68. How did you decide on how should you dress for the Program Manager interview?

69. Did you have a chance to apply what you learned on

the Program Manager job?

70. How would you describe the Program Manager office culture?

71. Whats the most recent mistake you made, and why did you make it?

72. What's the most difficult Program Manager decision you've made in the last two years and how did you come to that Program Manager decision?

73. What Program Manager challenges did you face in your last position?

74. Pick any event in the last five Program Manager years of your work which gives a good example of your ability to use forecasting techniques. Did you use statistical procedures or a gut level approach?

75. Give me an Program Manager example of a time at work when you had to deal with unreasonable expectations of you. What parts of your behavior were mature and immature?

76. What would you do if an employee called in sick three Mondays in a row?

77. What interests you most about this Program Manager job?

78. What Can You Do for Us That Other Program Manager Candidates Cant?

79. Often individuals who are creative in one mode seem to have creative Program Manager skills in other areas.

How do you rate yourself in terms of creativity in the fields of art, writing, and music?

80. Would you be able to meet this requirement?

81. Tell me about a Program Manager situation in which you were particularly skillful in detecting clues which show how another person thinks or feels. How did you size up the person?

82. What type of position are you looking for?

83. Describe a time when you went the extra mile for a Program Manager customer?

84. What was one of the worst Program Manager communication problems you have experienced?

85. Were you discharged under honorable or other acceptable Program Manager conditions?

86. How many days were you absent last year?

87. What sources would you use to research a Program Manager company for a potential job interview?

88. What s your availability for employment?

89. Give an Program Manager example of a difficult situation you had with a client or vendor?

90. What makes you unique?

91. How has your previous experience prepared you for the duties of this position?

92. How would you describe your interpersonal Program Manager communication skills?

93. Tell us about a time that others Program Manager actions negatively impacted a project for which you were responsible. What did you do?

94. To what extent has your past work required you to be skilled in the analysis of technical reports or Program Manager information?

95. What would you say about your ability to work in an ambiguous or unstructured circumstance?

96. Tell of some situations in which you have had to adjust quickly to changes over which you had no control. What was the impact of the change on you?

97. Describe the last time you confronted a peer about something he/she did that bothered you. What were the circumstances?

98. How many times have you totally altered behavior or belief in response to one persuasive Program Manager effort?

99. Have you ever worked on a project outside your Program Manager area of expertise?

100. Were you honorably discharged?

101. What does your spouse do for a living?

102. What major Program Manager accomplishment would you like to achieve in your life and why?

103. Has your Program Manager manager/supervisor/ team leader ever asked you to do something that you didnt think was appropriate?

104. Give me an Program Manager example of a time when you used a systematic process to define your objectives. What type of system did you use?

105. Your next question?

106. When have you found it necessary to use detailed checklists/Program Manager procedures to reduce potential for error on the job?

107. Tell me about a time when you were successful in this Program Manager area-what kind of payoffs accrued to yourself, the other individual, and the organization?

108. Describe what Program Manager steps/methods you have used to define/identify a vision for your unit/ position. How do you see your job relating to the overall goals of the organization?

109. When have you been most proud of your ability to wait for important Program Manager information before taking action in solving a problem?

110. Can you think of some Program Manager projects or ideas that were sold, implemented, or carried out successfully because of your efforts?

111. How much alcohol do you drink each week?

112. Give me a specific Program Manager example of a time when you had to address an angry customer. What was the problem and what was the outcome?

113. Did you use any tools such as research, brainstorming, or mathematics?

114. How would your past supervisors describe you?

115. Can you give me a specific Program Manager example from your past jobs or other experiences where you had to set priorities and plan your work?

116. What clubs, lodges do you belong to?

117. Tell me about a time you saw someone at work stretch or bend the rules beyond what you felt was acceptable. What did you do?

118. Why did you leave your last position?

119. Can you describe a time when your work was criticized?

120. What part did you play in helping a Program Manager group develop a final decision?

121. What are your strong Program Manager points?

122. What are your greatest Program Manager strengths?

123. What specific Program Manager goals, including those related to your occupation, have you established for your life?

124. If you were at a Program Manager business lunch and you ordered a rare steak and they brought it to you well done, what would you do?

125. Have you gone above and beyond the call of duty?

126. Some people consider themselves to be big Program Manager picture people and others are detail oriented. Which are you?

127. Describe a time when you got co-workers who dislike each other to work together. How did you accomplish this?

128. How did you ensure that the other person understood?

129. How much reading of new Program Manager information is required in your current job?

130. How did your planning help you deal with the unexpected?

131. How many people live in your household?

132. How many Program Manager employees did you supervise in your last job?

133. What type of supervisor works best for you?

134. Can you travel?

135. Are you bilingual?

136. Cite an Program Manager example where you had to delegate authority?

137. Describe a time when politics at work affected your Program Manager job. How did you handle the situation?

138. How would your Program Manager manager describe your performance?

139. Give an Program Manager example of when you questioned the way things have always been done to ensure that a process continued to be relevant and add value. What was the outcome?

140. What assignment was too difficult for you, and how did you resolve the Program Manager issue?

141. Tell me about a Program Manager customer whose needs you spent considerable time learning about. What was the result of the time investment?

142. What prior work experience have you had and how does it relate to this Program Manager job?

143. In which Program Manager kind of interviews have you participated?

144. If you could create your ideal Program Manager job, what Program Manager job would you create?

145. How do you know whether its better to lay out very specifically what others have to do – versus allowing them to use their own initiative and creativity?

146. What were your most significant accomplishments in your prior work experience?

147. You come across an online photo of an individual who works for you and his photo has something hanging out of his mouth that certainly looks like a marijuana cigarette Can you fire him?

148. What do you wish to avoid in your next Program Manager job?

149. What Program Manager types of experience have you had in managing situations that involve human health/human welfare or severe financial outcomes?

150. Tell me about a time you had to juggle a number of work priorities. What did you do?

151. What if someone on your Program Manager team isnt pulling their weight on a project and its affecting the speed and quality of the project...?

152. Tell me about a time when you handled an arrogant person or one who made you angry. What is your typical Program Manager way of dealing with conflict?

153. What computer software programs are you familiar with?

154. Did you ever serve in the armed forces of another

country?

155. Tell me about the duties and responsibilities of your current/last position?

156. How do you track your progress so that you can meet deadlines?

157. What are your greatest achievements at this point in your Program Manager life?

158. What advice do you wish you had been given when you were starting out?

159. Where do you live?

160. Describe the biggest challenge you ever faced?

161. What would be the best Program Manager example that shows you are an honest person?

162. Have you given out any _____?

163. Tell me about the specific times in which you have initiated your own Program Manager goal setting over the last few years. What happened?

164. When did you graduate from high school?

165. Describe the Program Manager system you use for keeping track of multiple projects. How do you track your progress so that you can meet deadlines?

166. What do you do if you disagree with your Program Manager boss?

167. Analyze your own Program Manager background. What skills do you have (content, functional, and adaptive) that relate to your job objective?

168. Select a Program Manager job you have had and describe the paperwork you were required to complete. What specific things did you do to ensure your accuracy?

169. Ive given you a short overview of the Program Manager job, but is there anything else that youd like to ask about?

170. Can you do the Program Manager job?

171. Give me a specific Program Manager example of a time when a co-worker or criticized your work in front of others. How did you respond?

172. I have a Program Manager job. I have a career. Im on a mission. Whats the difference between those three statements, and which one applies to you?

173. How did you define and measure Program Manager success?

174. Tell me about the biggest risk you ever took?

175. If you think about when you need high Program Manager performance, what behavior do you fall back on?

176. Have you ever been on welfare?

177. Would you be able and willing to travel as needed on this Program Manager job?

178. How would you address an angry Program Manager customer?

179. Describe how your position contributes to your organizations/units Program Manager goals. What are the units Program Manager goals/mission?

180. What was your greatest Program Manager success in using the principles of logic to solve technical problems at work?

181. Can you give me an Program Manager example of how you have persuaded executives to see your point of view in the past?

182. Can you give us an Program Manager example of when your curiosity made a real difference in a product or project?

183. Describe your ideal Program Manager candidate?

184. What was the most difficult Program Manager decision you have made in the last year?

185. What was your rank at time of discharge?

186. What specific Program Manager details should you identify when researching a company?

187. What was the most stressful Program Manager situation at work that you have faced?

188. Have you ever been arrested?

189. Have you ever legally changed your name?

190. How would you describe our organizational Program Manager culture?

191. What would be the best Program Manager example that shows you are a person of integrity?

192. Tell me about a time when you were asked to complete a difficult assignment and the odds were against you. What did you learn from the experience?

193. Have you ever led a research Program Manager team in a formal manner?

194. Describe a time when you had to influence a number of different constituents with differing interests. What Program Manager kind of influencing techniques did you use?

195. Describe a time you had to Program Manager delegate parts of a large project or assignment to some of your direct reports. How did you decide what tasks to Program Manager delegate to which people?

196. What Program Manager communication strengths do you have that make you suited for this type of work?

197. Tell me about a Program Manager team member from whom it was tough to get cooperation. How did you handle the situation?

198. If I were your supervisor and asked you to do something that you disagreed with, what would you do?

199. Why Do You Want to Work Here?

200. Do you have a list of potential Program Manager references?

201. When do you plan to retire?

202. Provide Program Manager examples of when results didn[1]t turn out as you planned. What did you do then?

203. What characteristics would you be looking for in the successful Program Manager job applicant?

204. Has poor motivation on someone elses part ever damaged anything you were trying to accomplish?

205. How many days were you out sick last year?

206. Tell me about the last time you had to sell your Program Manager ideas to others. What did you do that was particularly effective/ineffective?

207. Recall a time from your work experience when your Program Manager manager or supervisor was unavailable and a problem arose. What was the nature of the problem?

208. What are your Program Manager career plans (short

and long range)?

209. What are some of the objectives you would like accomplished in the next two or three months?

210. When have you been a part of a Program Manager team that drove an important business change?

211. Tell me about the most creative thing you ve ever done?

212. Give me an Program Manager example of a group decision you were involved with recently. What part did you play in helping the group develop the final decision?

213. Have you ever had to present an unpopular proposal/point of view that you believed in?

214. Tell me about a time when you failed to meet a deadline. What Program Manager things did you fail to do?

215. What are your short and long-Program Manager term goals?

216. What was the best Program Manager idea you had for improving the way things were done on your last job?

217. How have your extracurricular Program Manager activities and/or work experience prepared you for work in our company?

218. How did you prepare for this?

219. Can you perform these Program Manager tasks?

220. How would you describe yourself in Program Manager terms of your ability to work as a member of a team?

221. Why Did You Leave (Are You Leaving) Your Program Manager Job?

222. How do you motivate others to do a particularly good Program Manager job?

223. What were your favorite courses?

224. Is there any Program Manager day of the week youre not able to work?

225. Program Manager Jobs differ in the extent to which unexpected changes can disrupt daily responsibilities. How do you feel when this happens?

226. Do you feel that you have experienced a Behavioral Based Program Manager Interview yet?

227. What Program Manager things in your job give you a sense of accomplishment?

228. What have been your Program Manager experiences in defining long range goals?

229. Describe the last time you organized a project on the Program Manager job?

230. Make a list of your selling Program Manager points. What are your strengths, weaknesses, interests and

career goals?

231. What were the Program Manager Results of your actions?

232. Do you have any back Program Manager problems?

233. Please give us an Program Manager example when you met a tight deadline?

234. Tell me about a time when you had more on you plate than you could handle. How did you get everything accomplished?

235. Have you found Program Manager ways to make your job easier?

236. Describe how you would handle a Program Manager situation if you were required to finish multiple tasks by the end of the day, and there was no conceivable way that you could finish them.

237. How many children do you have?

238. Based on your prior work, what Program Manager ideas for improvement do you have?

239. Give an Program Manager example of when you planned how to eliminate unnecessary activities and procedures in order to improve efficiency and make better use of resources. What was the outcome of your efforts?

240. How have you positively changed in the workplace to adapt to your colleagues or supervisor?

241. Why are you interested in this particular Program Manager company?

242. What is your typical Program Manager way of dealing with conflict?

243. Have you ever had to work with, or for, someone who lied to you in the past?

244. What important Program Manager target dates did you set to reach objectives on your last job?

245. Can you tell us about a time when you needed to be particularly sensitive to another persons beliefs, cultural Program Manager background, or way of doing things?

246. Did you use statistical Program Manager procedures or a gut level approach?

247. Have you ever over-Program Manager planned a project or spent too much time in planning versus execution?

248. Describe a time when you were asked to complete a difficult Program Manager task or project where the odds were against you. Were you successful?

249. Can you recall a particularly stressful Program Manager situation you have had at work recently?

250. Where does your spouse work?

251. Describe for me your most recent Program Manager

group effort?

252. When have you had to cope with the anger or hostility of another person?

253. Who was your best client?

254. Is there something in this Program Manager job that you hope to accomplish that you were not able to accomplish in your last Program Manager job?

255. Have you had any prior work injuries?

256. Give an Program Manager example of when you had to work with someone who was difficult to get along with. Why was this person difficult?

257. How would you evaluate your technical Program Manager skills?

258. What Program Manager kind of experience do you have dealing with a heavy workload?

259. Did you have a strategic plan?

260. What specific Program Manager goals have you established for your career?

261. What disabilities and Program Manager challenges (physical, mental, emotional, or behavioral) can you comfortably handle?

262. What were your wages at your prior Program Manager job?

263. What do you expect from a Program Manager

manager?

264. Please tell me about accomplishments in your academic Program Manager program that are relevant to your future career goals?

265. What has been your experience in working with conflicting, delayed, or ambiguous Program Manager information?

266. How do you go about establishing rapport with a student or Program Manager customer?

267. Give me an Program Manager example of when you had to show good leadership?

268. How do you react to criticism?

269. What made your Program Manager communication effective?

270. What is the biggest mistake youve made?

271. Give me a specific Program Manager example of a time when you had to work with a difficult customer?

272. Give me a specific Program Manager example of a time when you sold your supervisor or professor on an idea or concept. How did you proceed?

273. Tell me about the last time you had to smooth over a disagreement between two other people. What was the end result?

274. Why should you hire you?

275. In your last or current Program Manager job, what problems did you identify that had previously been overlooked?

276. Tell me about a Program Manager situation in which you worked with your direct reports/team members to develop new and creative ideas to solve a business problem. What problem were you trying to solve?

277. Tell me about the most difficult or uncooperative person you had to work with lately. What did you do or say to resolve the Program Manager situation?

278. Have you ever managed multiple Program Manager projects simultaneously?

279. How do you keep your Program Manager staff informed of what s going on in the organization?

280. What are you looking for in your next Program Manager career opportunity?

281. What are your Program Manager standards of success/goals for a job?

282. What is your initial reaction to change?

283. How Do You Know When You ve Got It Right?

284. How did you get everything accomplished?

285. Tell me about a time you had a particularly difficult Program Manager problem to solve. What was the Program Manager problem, how did you solve it, or what was the result?

286. Give me an Program Manager example of a time you did something wrong. How did you handle it?

287. What Program Manager kinds of decisions do you make rapidly and which ones to you take more time on?

288. Have you ever been in a Program Manager situation where, although it was difficult for you, you were honest and told the truth, and suffered negative consequences?

289. What did you do that was particularly effective/ineffective?

290. What are the most challenging documents you have done?

291. Tell me about a Program Manager task or project that you unsuccessfully delegated. What happened?

292. Are you in good physical condition?

293. Give an Program Manager example of how you worked effectively with people to accomplish an important result. Have you ever been a project leader?

294. Tell me about a Program Manager suggestion you

made to improve the way job processes or operations worked. What was the result?

295. What have you done when your schedule was interrupted on the Program Manager job?

296. Tell me about a time when your attempt to motivate a person/Program Manager group was rejected. What have you done to remotivate a demoralized team/person?

297. Why are you interested in this position?

298. Describe a time when you were faced with Program Manager problems or stresses at work that tested your coping skills. What did you do?

299. What Program Manager skills do you have (content, functional, and adaptive) that relate to your job objective?

300. Describe a Program Manager situation where others you were working with on a project disagreed with your ideas. What did you do?

301. Give an Program Manager example of a time when you made a mistake. How did you handle it?

302. In what areas do you find yourself procrastinating?

303. Describe a time when you were expected to act in accordance with Program Manager policy even when it was not convenient. What did you do?

304. Tell me about a time when you postponed making a

Program Manager decision. Why did you?

305. What Are Three Positive Program Manager Things Your Last Supervisor Would Say About You?

306. What led you to select your Program Manager college major?

307. Tell me about a time you had to say no to a Program Manager customer?

308. What did you do in your last Program Manager job to contribute toward a teamwork environment?

309. We all have to make Program Manager decisions on the job about the delicate balance between personal and work objectives. When do you feel you have had to make personal sacrifices in order to get the job done?

310. When have you found yourself in my position?

311. Tell me about a time when you had to take care of an upset Program Manager customer?

312. What was the most difficult Program Manager period in your life, and how did you deal with it?

313. What are your Program Manager career goals in the next 3-5 years?

314. What motivates you to put forth your greatest Program Manager effort?

315. What prompted your interest in our position?

316. Describe a time when you had to adopt a well-defined work Program Manager routine. How long did the situation last?

317. What Program Manager skills do you bring to the job?

318. What schools have you attended and when?

319. What language do you speak at home?

320. How would you describe the quality and quantity of his/her work?

321. Tell me about the Program Manager system that you use for goal setting. To what extent does it involve using written objectives, paper work or forms?

322. On a scale of 0-10, how confident are you that you can change successfully?

323. What are your Program Manager career interests?

324. How do you determine or evaluate Program Manager success?

325. What are your Program Manager strengths/weaknesses?

326. Tell me about a time when you came up with an innovative Program Manager solution to a challenge

your company / organization was facing. What was the challenge?

327. Tell Me About Yourself?

328. Describe the last time you were criticized by a peer or supervisor. How did you handle it?

329. What significant changes do you foresee in the Program Manager company / organization?

330. What specific Program Manager things did you do to ensure your accuracy?

331. Do you prefer to work independently or on a Program Manager team?

332. When you worked on multiple Program Manager projects how did you prioritize?

333. How does your graduate school experience relate to this Program Manager job?

334. What is the worst mistake you ever made?

335. What additional Program Manager information would you like me to provide?

336. Have you ever faced a Program Manager problem you could not solve?

337. How would you describe your Program Manager management style?

338. What Program Manager steps do you take in preparing for a meeting where you are attempting to

persuade someone on a specific course of action?

339. Tell me about a time when your carefully laid plans were fouled up. What happened?

340. How would you feel supervising two or three other Program Manager employees?

341. If you had to describe yourself, what Program Manager words would you use?

342. What did you do or say to resolve a Program Manager situation?

343. Have you received any _____?

344. What are your areas of strength?

345. Have you ever had to manage a Program Manager team that was not up to the task?

346. Did you take Program Manager action IMMEDIATELY or are you more DELIBERATE and slow?

347. Tell me about times when you seized the opportunities, grabbed something and ran with it yourself. Have you ever started something up from nothing – give an Program Manager example?

348. What is your timetable for achievement of your current Program Manager career goals?

349. Describe the Program Manager types of teams youve been involved with. What were your roles?

350. Give an Program Manager example to a time when you encountered a difficult situation with a co-worker?

351. Have you ever taken a stand or said something in public that you knew those above you would not like?

352. What do you know about our Program Manager Company and/or the position for which you are applying?

353. List all organizations to which you belong. Were you ever a union Program Manager member?

354. Describe a time when you put your needs aside to help a co-worker understand a Program Manager task. How did you assist him or her?

355. What was the last project you led, and what was its Program Manager outcome?

356. What, in your Program Manager opinion, are the key ingredients in guiding and maintaining successful business relationships?

357. Give an Program Manager example of a time when you had a conflict with a supervisor?

358. Do you own a car?

359. What will it take to attain your Program Manager goals, and what steps have you taken toward attaining them?

360. What Program Manager effort does handling many things simultaneously have on you?

361. What situations do you find most frustrating?

362. Have you ever designed a Program Manager program which dealt with taking quicker action?

363. What Program Manager problem were you trying to solve?

364. Time Program Manager management has become a necessary factor in personal productivity. Give me an example of any Time Program Manager management skill you have learned and applied at work. What resulted from use of the skill?

365. Do you have any health Program Manager problems?

366. How would you resolve a Program Manager customer service problem where the Program Manager customer demanded an immediate refund?

367. What, if anything, did you do to mitigate the negative consequences to people?

368. How would you organize your Program Manager friends to help you move into a new apartment?

369. What type of Program Manager system did you use?

370. What attracts you to this particular Program Manager industry?

371. How would you deal with an angry Program Manager customer?

372. Give me an Program Manager example of a time that you felt you went above and beyond the call of duty at work.

373. Whats the origin of your name?

374. How do you handle stress and Program Manager pressure on the job?

375. Were you ever a union Program Manager member?

376. Describe a specific Program Manager problem you solved for your employer. How did you approach the Program Manager problem?

377. Have you ever dealt with Program Manager company policy you werent in agreement with?

378. What rewards are most important to you in your Program Manager career and why?

379. Describe a significant project Program Manager idea you initiated in the last year. How did you know it was needed?

380. Did you do anything specific to deal with the stress?

381. Are you decisive on the Program Manager job?

382. Give me an Program Manager example of a time you had to make an important decision. How did you make the decision?

383. If you found out your Program Manager company was doing something against the law, like fraud, what would you do?

384. Where do you want to be five Program Manager years from now?

385. How do you determine what is right or fair in delegating Program Manager tasks / roles / responsibilities within your organization?

386. Can you tell us about a time when you formed an ongoing working Program Manager relationship or partnership with someone from another organization to achieve a mutual goal?

387. How did you decide what Program Manager tasks to delegate to which people?

388. Why do you think you would be good at this Program Manager job

389. What are your major Program Manager strengths and weaknesses?

390. Tell me about the most frustrating thing you ever had to deal with?

391. Have you had any personal, domestic or financial Program Manager problems that interfered with your work?

Stress Management

1. How did you react when faced with constant time Program Manager pressure? Give an example

2. What Program Manager kind of events cause you stress on the job?

3. People react differently when Program Manager job demands are constantly changing; how do you react?

4. What was the most stressful Program Manager situation you have faced? How did you deal with it?

Adaptability

1. How do different project Program Manager types, procurement routes, clients, and/ or locations influence your pull?

2. Tell us about a Program Manager situation in which you had to adjust to changes over which you had no control. How did you handle it?

3. Tell me about a time when you failed. Why did it happen? What did you do next and what would you do differently if given another chance?

4. What was your biggest Program Manager failure?

5. How do you know if an Program Manager organization is adaptable?

6. Tell me about the first Program Manager job you've ever had. What did you do to learn the ropes?

7. What is your greatest Program Manager failure, and what did you learn from it?

8. Give me an Program Manager example of a time when you had to think on your feet in order to delicately extricate yourself from a difficult or awkward situation.

9. What Program Manager role should a hobby play in this job interview?

10. How might a lateral move help you get the promotion?

11. What are the licensing, certifications, and credentialing Program Manager requirements for this job?

12. What ongoing professional Program Manager development opportunities exist in this career?

13. What Program Manager skills, activities and attitudes lead to promotion?

14. What is your biggest work related Program Manager failure in the last six months and how did you overcome it?

15. In your chosen work Program Manager area, what are five careers that seem attractive to you?

16. How many times have you failed?

17. Tell me about two memorable Program Manager projects, one success and one failure. To what do you attribute the success and failure?

18. Is ours a learning Program Manager organization?

19. When does a hobby start to become work?

20. What is your biggest Program Manager career screw-up?

21. How do Program Manager leaders develop organizations capable of adapting in the volatile, uncertain, complex, and ambiguous environment envisioned by senior Program Manager leaders?

22. What is the meaning of Adaptability in the Program Manager industry?

23. Do you have enough stress to make you ill?

24. Describe a time when you failed to engage at the right level in your Program Manager organization. Why did you do that and how did you handle the situation?

25. What's your biggest Program Manager failure - why is it a Program Manager failure and what did you learn from it?

26. Are you a resilient survivor?

27. What Program Manager kinds of educational decisions make you more promotable?

28. When the unexpected happens what next?

29. How can a hobby prepare you for work?

30. What other occupations also require your Program Manager skills?

31. Tell me about a time you were under a lot of Program Manager pressure. What was going on and how did you get through it?

32. What is meant by being more flexible?

33. In what Program Manager ways can you build on your present skills?

34. What careers would allow you to do what you really enjoy doing?

35. What professional organizations support your careers of interest?

36. Describe a major change that occurred in a Program Manager job that you held. How did you adapt to this change?

37. How must you adapt in your workplace in order to advance?

38. What do you do when priorities change quickly? Give one Program Manager example of when this happened

39. What Program Manager benefits do you get from belonging to this organization?

40. How would you create and then lead an Program Manager organization where the infrastructure is flexible, but yet efficient, effective, and reliable?

41. Describe a time when your Program Manager team or company was undergoing some change. How did that impact you, and how did you adapt?

42. Tell me about a time you failed. How did you deal with this Program Manager situation?

43. How do we foster a Program Manager culture that allows open dialog between everyone regardless of rank?

44. What s the long-Program Manager term plan beyond your first job at our company?

45. At what point do you engage/ step away?

46. If you do your Program Manager job well, will you automatically get promoted?

47. Tell us about a time that you had to adapt to a difficult Program Manager situation

48. How does one design for time?

Project Management

1. Tell us about a time when you Program Manager influenced the outcome of a project by taking a leadership role

2. Using a specific Program Manager example of a project, tell how you kept those involved informed of the progress

Introducing Change

1. Do you know what your Program Manager role could be in implementing a performance management system?

2. How have you articulated the reason for the change?

3. What Program Manager qualities do you possess that will lead us to nominate your over other candidates?

4. Were you able to do your Program Manager job as well as before after a major change?

5. What support are you getting from your Program Manager management team, sponsor etc?

6. What specific Program Manager actions are your managers taking to support you / your project?

7. How well managed did you think a major change was?

8. What media are you using for Program Manager communication, and what is most effective?

9. What disruption did you feel?

10. Do you understand the purpose of implementing a Program Manager performance management system?

11. What training did you receive?

12. Are you familiar with the content of a Program Manager performance management system?

13. How would you define the Program Manager culture (the way you do things around here) within your current work environment?

14. Have you ever met Program Manager resistance when implementing a new idea or policy to a work group? How did you deal with it? What happened?

15. Do people in your current work encourage each other to support the change initiatives within the organisation?

16. How do you propose to measure Program Manager performance or the achievement of any projects objectives?

17. Have you ever had to introduce a Program Manager policy change to your work group? How did you do it?

18. When is the last time you had to introduce a new Program Manager idea or procedure to people on this job? How did you do it?

19. What will you do to ensure that you will be able to transfer the Program Manager knowledge and skills obtained from your previous experiences to other colleagues?

Integrity

1. Describe a time when you were asked to keep Program Manager information confidential

2. On occasion we are confronted by dishonesty in the workplace. Tell about such an occurrence and how you handled it

3. Give Program Manager examples of how you have acted with integrity in your job/work relationship

4. Trust requires personal accountability. Can you tell about a time when you chose to trust someone? What was the Program Manager outcome?

5. Tell us about a specific time when you had to handle a tough Program Manager problem which challenged fairness or ethnical issues

6. If you can, tell about a time when your trustworthiness was challenged. How did you react/respond?

Interpersonal Skills

1. What does personal responsibility mean to you?

2. What is troubling you?

3. Do you nap during the Program Manager day?

4. What do you enjoy doing?

5. What keeps you going and/or gives you hope?

6. How did you feel?

7. Do you feel rested or not rested when you wake up?

8. How do you feel today?

9. In which areas are you satisfied or dissatisfied?

10. How many Program Manager hours do you sleep if you add them all up, even if they are interrupted?

11. What do you do well?

12. What does your Program Manager brain contain?

13. Self-regard is the ability to respect and accept oneself as you are. In which areas are you satisfied or

dissatisfied?

14. This Program Manager office is many times all things to all people. How do you see your skills and personality fitting into that expectation?

15. If you were forced to live under a different political régime that is very different from that which you know, what would be most important to you?

16. What would you save in the event of a disaster such as a fire or a flood?

17. If 1 = the worst and 10 = the best, how would you rate your sleep on average these days?

18. What makes one Program Manager day the best Program Manager day of your life?

19. Bad Program Manager things happen to people all the time in our world. What if they were to happen to you?

20. How would you handle Program Manager questions that go beyond your knowledge?

21. What Program Manager kind of supervision have you had in the past and how have you responded to it?

22. Tell us about the most difficult or frustrating individual that you've ever had to work with, and how you managed to work with them

23. At least how many people a week do you communicate with?

24. Have you ever been called a worrywart?

25. Question your own defensiveness. What Program Manager situation makes you upset?

26. What is the funniest thing that has ever happened to you?

27. Tell us how you have handled past work situations that required confidentiality. How might that Program Manager procedure impact this office?

28. Do you have a plan?

29. Did anything make you laugh today?

30. What have you done in past situations to contribute toward a teamwork Program Manager environment?

31. How many times have you tried to communicate with an Program Manager organization by phone and been left feeling really frustrated?

32. What is your understanding of the Program Manager word teamwork and how you have been involved with that process on the job or in other settings. How might teamwork (or lack of it) affect an office setting?

33. Spend a few minutes thinking about what the best Program Manager day of your life would be like. Then tell a story describing in detail everything about that Program Manager day. What makes this one Program Manager day the best Program Manager day of your life?

34. Which code of practice do you use to review your Program Manager performance?

35. Do you have any Program Manager questions of us about this position?

36. What causes you to lose your cool?

37. What might your current colleagues say about you and the Program Manager way you relate to others?

38. What have you done in the past to contribute toward a teamwork Program Manager environment?

39. Who is one of the funniest people you know?

40. What gives you strength?

41. Without taking the Program Manager problem on yourself, whom would you help and what Program Manager problems would you help them solve?

42. What are the most important Program Manager things in your life?

43. Are the beliefs that you have about yourself TRUE or FALSE?

44. How would you characterize my interpersonal Program Manager skills?

45. Describe a recent unpopular Program Manager

decision you made and what the result was

46. How do you see your Program Manager skills and personality fitting into our organization?

47. Are you doing what needs to be done to meet your Program Manager goals?

48. Do you have the confidence that you desire?

49. Evaluate your progress towards your Program Manager goals. Are you doing what needs to be done to meet your Program Manager goals?

50. Describe a Program Manager situation in which you were able to effectively 'read' another person and guide your actions by your understanding of their needs and values

51. Think of the person who knows you best; a person who knows both good and bad Program Manager things about your personality. What might they say about you and the way you relate to others?

Resolving Conflict

1. Tell us about a time when you had to help two peers settle a Program Manager dispute. How did you go about identifying the issues? What did you do? What was the result?

2. Describe a time when you took personal accountability for a conflict and initiated Program Manager contact with the individual(s) involved to explain your actions

3. Have you ever been in a Program Manager situation where you had to settle an argument between two friends (or people you knew)? What did you do? What was the result?

4. Have you ever had to settle conflict between two people on the Program Manager job? What was the situation and what did you do?

Reference

1. How do you and X know each other?

2. If I talked to your current/past Program Manager manager and asked them to describe you, what would they say?

3. Can you provide 2-3 Program Manager references that we could shoot a quick email to that would be ok sharing their experiences of working with you?

4. Who are your mentors and why?

Motivating Others

1. How do you get subordinates to produce at a high level? Give an Program Manager example

2. How do you deal with people whose work exceeds your expectations?

3. Have you ever had a subordinate whose work was always marginal? How did you deal with that person? What happened?

4. How do you manage cross-functional Program Manager teams?

5. How do you get subordinates to work at their Program Manager peak potential? Give an example

Teamwork

1. Some people work best as part of a Program Manager group - others prefer the role of individual contributor. How would you describe yourself? Give an example of a situation where you felt you were most effective

2. Tell us about a time that you had to work on a Program Manager team that did not get along. What happened? What role did you take? What was the result?

3. We all make Program Manager mistakes we wish we could take back. Tell me about a time you wish you'd handled a situation differently with a colleague.

4. Describe a time when you struggled to build a Program Manager relationship with someone important. How did you eventually overcome that?

5. Describe a Program Manager team experience you found rewarding

6. What Program Manager role have you typically played as a member of a team? How did you interact with other members of the team?

7. Please give your best Program Manager example of working cooperatively as a team member to accomplish an important goal What was the goal or objective? To what extent did you interact with others on this project?

8. Tell us about the most effective Program Manager

contribution you have made as part of a task group or special project team

9. Describe your Program Manager leadership style and give an example of a situation when you successfully led a group

10. Have you ever participated in a Program Manager task group? What was your role? How did you contribute?

11. Tell us about the most difficult challenge you faced in trying to work cooperatively with someone who did not share the same Program Manager ideas? What was your role in achieving the work objective?

12. Think about the times you have been a Program Manager team leader. What could you have done to be more effective?

13. Describe a Program Manager situation in which you had to arrive at a compromise or help others to compromise. What was your role? What steps did you take? What was the end result?

14. Tell us about the most difficult Program Manager situation you have had when leading a team. What happened and what did you do? Was it successful? Emphasize the 'single' most important thing you did?

15. Have you ever been in a position where you had to lead a Program Manager group of peers? How did you handle it?

16. Describe the Program Manager types of teams you've

been involved with. What were your roles?

17. Tell me about a time you needed to get Program Manager information from someone who wasn't very responsive. What did you do?

18. Give me an Program Manager example of a time you faced a conflict while working on a team. How did you handle that?

19. Tell us about a work experience where you had to work closely with others. How did it go? How did you overcome any Program Manager difficulties?

20. Talk about a time when you had to work closely with someone whose Program Manager personality was very different from yours.

21. Have you ever been a project Program Manager leader? Give examples of problems you experienced and how you reacted

22. Give an Program Manager example of how you worked effectively with people to accomplish an important result

23. What is the difficult part of being a Program Manager member, not leader, of a team? How did you handle this?

24. When working on a Program Manager team project have you ever had an experience where there was strong disagreement among Program Manager team members? What did you do?

25. Describe a Program Manager team experience you

found disappointing. What would you have done to prevent this?

26. When is the last time you had a disagreement with a peer? How did you resolve the Program Manager situation?

27. Give an Program Manager example of how you have been successful at empowering a group of people in accomplishing a task

Career Development

1. If you found out your Program Manager company was doing something against the law, like fraud, what would you do?

2. What magazines do you subscribe to?

3. What Program Manager qualities do you feel a successful manager should have?

4. What Program Manager education is required for your chosen career?

5. How have you gone above and beyond the call of duty?

6. Whats the last Program Manager book you read?

7. How would you describe your work Program Manager style?

8. What were your Program Manager bosses strengths/weaknesses?

9. What do you like to do for Program Manager fun?

10. What Program Manager kind of personality do you work best with and why?

11. What negative thing would your last Program Manager boss say about you?

12. What Program Manager techniques and tools do you

use to keep yourself organized?

13. Why was there a Program Manager gap in your employment between insert date and insert date?

14. Do you think a Program Manager leader should be feared or liked?

15. Identify what is unique or special about you. How have you gone above and beyond the call of duty?

16. What is your personal Program Manager mission statement?

17. What are your Program Manager skills?

18. Was there a person in your Program Manager career who really made a difference?

19. How would you define a positive work Program Manager environment?

20. Why should I hire you?

21. If you were interviewing someone for this position, what traits would you look for?

22. How would you feel about working for someone who knows less than you?

23. What do you want to be?

24. In thinking about your Program Manager future, you must consider whats important to you in your daily life.

What would you think about a career that required a great deal of travel?

25. How can YOU monitor your Program Manager data?

26. What are some aspects of your present Program Manager job that you enjoy / dislike?

27. Give me an Program Manager example of a time you did something wrong. How did you handle it?

28. Have you ever been on a Program Manager team where someone was not pulling their weight?

29. What are your interests?

30. Who do you serve?

31. Why did you apply to this position?

32. What is your favorite Program Manager memory from childhood?

33. Whats your availability?

34. Whats the most difficult Program Manager decision youve made in the last two years and how did you come to that Program Manager decision?

35. Theres no right or wrong answer, but if you could be anywhere in the Program Manager world right now, where would you be?

36. What is your greatest Program Manager weakness?

37. Who are your collaborators?

38. What are three positive Program Manager character traits you dont have?

39. How would you define a positive work Program Manager environment?

40. Related occupation: Are there other Program Manager career fields/occupations that look like a good match for you?

41. What specific Program Manager steps did you take and what was your particular contribution?

42. What is your greatest Program Manager failure, and what did you learn from it?

43. Did you think about what the Program Manager outcome should be?

44. Have you ever had a conflict with a Program Manager boss or professor?

45. What was the last project you headed up, and what was its Program Manager outcome?

46. What Program Manager questions havent I asked you?

47. What would you think about a Program Manager career that required a great deal of travel?

48. What do you look for in Program Manager terms of culture -- structured or entrepreneurial?

49. What was the last project you led, and what was its Program Manager outcome?

50. If you could choose one superhero Program Manager power, what would it be and why?

51. Have you ever been on a Program Manager team where someone was not pulling their own weight?

52. Whats the most important thing you learned in school?

53. How do you think I rate as an interviewer?

54. What do your reports reflect?

55. What are your lifelong Program Manager dreams?

56. How much do outside influences play a Program Manager role in your job performance?

57. How long will it take you to make a Program Manager contribution?

58. What Program Manager kind of goals would you have in mind if you got this job?

59. If I were to ask your last supervisor to provide you additional training or Program Manager exposure, what would she suggest?

60. How do you want to improve yourself in the next year?

61. How do you feel about taking no for an answer?

62. What do you see yourself doing 5 or 10 Program Manager years from now?

63. What were the responsibilities of your last position?

64. What Program Manager kind of goals would you have in mind if you got this job?

65. What was the most difficult Program Manager period in your life, and how did you deal with it?

66. Who reviews your Program Manager data?

67. What three Program Manager character traits would your friends use to describe you?

68. How do you prepare for the Program Manager career?

69. What would be your ideal working Program Manager environment?

70. What is your greatest achievement outside of work?

71. Whats the best Program Manager movie youve seen in the last year?

72. What do you know about this Program Manager industry?

73. Can you describe a time when your work was criticized?

74. Why did you choose your major?

75. What is your biggest regret and why?

76. Who was your favorite Program Manager manager and why?

77. If you had to choose one, would you consider yourself a big-Program Manager picture person or a detail-oriented person?

78. What is your plan for competency attainment?

79. What irritates you about other people, and how do you deal with it?

80. What are you looking for in Program Manager terms of career development?

81. Who has impacted you most in your Program Manager career and how?

82. What is your greatest fear?

83. What does your appearance say about you?

84. Are you a Program Manager team player?

85. What do you look for in Program Manager terms of culture -structured or entrepreneurial?

86. Whats your ideal Program Manager company?

87. What do you ultimately want to become?

88. Program Manager Education and/or training after high school: What colleges or training programs did you attend to prepare for your preferred occupations?

89. What Program Manager kind of car do you drive?

90. What Program Manager types of careers fit your skills and interest?

91. How do you handle working with people who annoy you?

92. What will you miss about your present/last Program Manager job?

93. What do you like to do?

94. What do you think of your previous Program Manager boss?

95. What else besides your schooling and experience qualify you for this Program Manager job?

96. What do you do in your spare time?

97. What would you do if you won the lottery?

98. What would be your ideal working Program Manager situation?

99. What is your Program Manager Career Goal?

100. Worried Youre In A Dead-End Program Manager Job?

101. How would you feel about a Program Manager job that required you to move on a regular basis?

102. What are your interest?

103. What assignment was too difficult for you, and how did you resolve the Program Manager issue?

104. Whos your Program Manager mentor?

105. What are three positive Program Manager things your last boss would say about you?

106. What are you looking for in Program Manager terms of career development?

Relate Well

1. Describe a Program Manager situation where you had to use conflict management skills

2. Give me an Program Manager example of a time when a company policy or action hurt people. What, if anything, did you do to mitigate the negative consequences to people?

3. Describe a Program Manager situation where you had to use confrontation skills

4. What would your co-workers (or Program Manager staff) stay is the most frustrating thing about your communications with them?

5. Tell us about a time when you were forced to make an unpopular Program Manager decision

6. How do you typically deal with conflict? Can you give me an Program Manager example?

Evaluating Alternatives

1. How did you assemble the Program Manager information?

2. How did you review the Program Manager information? What process did you follow to reach a conclusion?

3. What are some of the major Program Manager decisions you have made over the past (6, 12, 18) months?

4. What alternatives did you develop?

5. Have you ever had a Program Manager situation where you had a number of alternatives to choose from? How did you go about choosing one?

6. What Program Manager kinds of decisions are most difficult for you? Describe one?

Performance Management

1. Tell us about a time when you had to take disciplinary Program Manager action with someone you supervised

2. There are times when people need extra help. Give an Program Manager example of when you were able to provide that support to a person with whom you worked

3. Tell us about a training Program Manager program that you have developed or enhanced

4. Tell us about a time when you had to tell a Program Manager staff member that you were dissatisfied with his or her work

5. How often do you discuss a subordinate's Program Manager performance with him/her? Give an example

6. How do you handle Program Manager performance reviews? Tell me about a difficult one

7. Give an Program Manager example of how you have been successful at empowering either a person or a group of people into accomplishing a task

8. When do you give positive Program Manager feedback to people? Tell me about the last time you did. Give an example of how you handle the need for constructive criticism with a subordinate or peer

9. What have you done to develop the Program Manager

skills of your staff?

10. Tell us about a time when you had to use your authority to get something done. Where there any negative consequences?

11. Tell us about a specific Program Manager development plan that you created and carried out with one or more of your employees What was the specific situation? What were the components of the Program Manager development plan? What was the outcome?

12. How do you handle a subordinate whose work is not up to expectations?

13. Give an Program Manager example of a time when you helped a staff member accept change and make the necessary adjustments to move forward. What were the change/transition skills that you used

14. How do you coach a subordinate to develop a new Program Manager skill?

Negotiating

1. What do you need me to feel?

2. Where might your interests and the interests of the opposite coincide?

3. Will you make the first offer?

4. How do you say yes, no, and maybe?

5. Do you send the Program Manager information piecemeal, or wait to collect all the Program Manager information and send one bill?

6. What do you need to learn?

7. From your Program Manager perspective, what are the overarching issues?

8. Identify your stakeholders. What are the stakeholders positions and interests?

9. Is there an Program Manager action you can take to help develop trust (provide information, demonstrate sincerity)?

10. What changes were you able to accommodate and why?

11. Who can influence the Program Manager outcome of the talks, besides the one(s) you will negotiate with?

12. How does the salary match the research you did and your Program Manager range?

13. Closure – how do you plan on converting from divergent thinking (option Program Manager development) to convergent thinking (solution selection)?

14. Do you have any Program Manager questions?

15. Are there any Time Bombs in your proposed offers?

16. How did you resolve it?

17. What lessons can you extract from this negotiation to help Program Manager mentor others?

18. What is your walk away point?

19. How did you present your position?

20. Sequencing – How do you want to sequentially organize your negotiation?

21. What is your assessment of the level of trust between you and the opposite?

22. What will your opening statement be the first 90 seconds?

23. What should you do if you have no alternatives to agreement and the other side is big and powerful?

24. What Program Manager questions/answers about the other side might strengthen your position during

negotiations and thus increase your chances of a successful outcome?

25. Your BATNA?

26. How do you call an intermission?

27. Which matters most to you?

28. What was the most difficult part?

29. How do you prepare for a negotiation?

30. How much will you ask for?

31. Are the offers at least as good as your best Alternative to negotiated agreement?

32. What if the other side plays dirty, how should you respond?

33. Why are they talking to you?

34. How did you prepare for it?

35. Have you ever been in a Program Manager situation where you had to bargain with someone? How did you feel about this? What did you do? Give an example

36. Do the offers satisfy the Interests youve listed?

37. Is there anything else you can do in Program Manager terms of the offer?

38. Tell us about the last time you had to negotiate with someone

39. Describe the most challenging negotiation in which you were involved. What did you do? What were the Program Manager results for you? What were the Program Manager results for the other party?

40. Will the salary meet your needs?

41. Have you ever had the need to help your Program Manager group get on the same page to manage a conflict, ready for a transaction, or make a decision?

42. What do you think they want the Program Manager situation to be AFTER the negotiations conclude (what is/are the opposites perceptions of longterm interest(s))?

43. Ask yourself what they other Program Manager sides BATNA may be. Why are they talking to you?

44. What aspect of this negotiation was most challenging for you?

45. What does your Program Manager organization / chain of command / team want to have happen?

46. Reservation Point: What is the least you are willing to accept?

Sound Judgment

1. When have you had to produce Program Manager results without sufficient guidelines? Give an example

2. Give me an Program Manager example of a time in which you had to be relatively quick in coming to a decision

3. We work with a great deal of confidential Program Manager information. Describe how you would have handled sensitive Program Manager information in a past work experience. What strategies would you utilize to maintain confidentiality when pressured by others?

4. Describe a Program Manager situation when you had to exercise a significant amount of self-control

5. If you were interviewing for this position what would you be looking for in the applicants?

6. Give me an Program Manager example of when you were responsible for an error or mistake. What was the outcome? What, if anything, would you do differently?

7. Give me an Program Manager example of when you were able to meet the personal and professional demands in your life yet still maintained a healthy balance

Strategic Planning

1. How do you see your Program Manager job relating to the overall goals of the organization?

2. Tell us about a time when you anticipated the Program Manager future and made changes to current responsibilities/operations to meet Program Manager future needs

3. In your current or former position, what were your long and short-Program Manager term goals?

4. Describe what Program Manager steps/methods you have used to define/identify a vision for your unit/position

Extracurricular

1. What are the three most interesting just-for-Program Manager fun projects you've built?

2. Have you ever created any side-Program Manager projects or organized any community events?

3. What's next on your Program Manager bucket list and why?

4. What do you do for Program Manager fun and what hobbies do you partake in when you are not at work?

5. What did you do in Program Manager college aside from going to school?

6. Based on all the facets of our Program Manager company (big data, unconscious bias, diversity, analytics, mobile apps, etc) what relevant work have you done OUTSIDE OF WORK?

7. Have you ever played a Program Manager team sport?

8. Identify a project or Program Manager task that you would be the most proud of and would consider your most significant accomplishment in your career to date and describe the circumstances. How you got involved, your contributions and participation along with your reasoning on why this is the one you picked?

Analytical Thinking

1. Relate a specific Program Manager instance when you found it necessary to be precise in your in order to complete the job

2. Do you know what the Program Manager outcome should be after you follow instructions?

3. Tell us about your experience in past Program Manager jobs that required you to be especially alert to details while doing the task involved

4. What do you do when the patterns break down?

5. How does this activity we're doing right now relate to learning?

6. Give me an Program Manager example of when you took a risk to achieve a goal. What was the outcome?

7. How did you go about making the changes (step by step)? Answer in Program Manager depth or detail such as 'What were you thinking at that point?' or 'Tell me more about meeting with that person', or 'Lead me through your decision process'

8. What is your approach to solving Program Manager problems?

9. Do you agree with author James Fixx, who asserts, In solving puzzles, a self-assured Program Manager attitude is half the battle?

10. What's the connection between hands and the ocean?

11. Tell us about a Program Manager job or setting where great precision to detail was required to complete a task. How did you handle that situation?

12. Describe the project or Program Manager situation which best demonstrates your analytical abilities. What was your role?

13. Do you ask yourself after every interaction with the Program Manager team, Have I left them feeling stronger and more capable than before?

14. What happens when you are called upon to make a statement on the spot, to make a Program Manager decision without having all the facts, to solve a problem that will only be exacerbated by delay?

15. How can we maximize the investment in your training, after the training?

16. What Program Manager techniques do you know of to stimulate free association or brainstorming?

17. How does this activity we're doing right now relate to thinking?

18. Which of our Managerial Competencies most support your personal Program Manager development goals?

19. In your current Program Manager job role, what energizes you?

20. Give me a specific Program Manager example of a time when you used good judgment and logic in solving a problem

21. What rules do you feel should be changed?

22. Developing and using a detailed Program Manager procedure is often very important in a job. Tell about a time when you needed to develop and use a detailed Program Manager procedure to successfully complete a project

23. What is your evaluation of the educational training at secondary level in our country?

24. Ever see the face of someone you know in a potato chip?

25. Should spent nuclear fuel be reprocessed?

26. What is the greatest Program Manager contribution you can make to this organization?

27. What is critical thinking and analytical thinking?

28. Tell us about a time when you had to analyze Program Manager information and make a recommendation. What kind of thought process did you go through? What was your reasoning behind your decision?

29. What do you think Tom Peters means when he says, If you have gone a whole week without being disobedient, you are doing yourself and your Program Manager organization a disservice?

30. What are you looking at that no one else can see?

31. What Program Manager resources, human and other, remain untapped in our organization?

Outgoingness

1. Tell us about a time when you had to motivate a Program Manager group of people to get an important job done. What did you do, what was the outcome?

2. Describe a time when you were able to effectively communicate a difficult or unpleasant Program Manager idea to a superior.

3. Being Program Manager successful is hard work. Tell us about a specific achievement when you had to work especially hard to attain the Program Manager success you desired.

4. There are times when we need to insist on doing something a certain Program Manager way. Give us the details surrounding a situation when you had to insist on doing something "your Program Manager way". What was the outcome?

5. Tell us about a time when you were effective in handling a Program Manager customer complaint. Why were you effective? What was the outcome?

6. Sooner or later we all have to deal with a Program Manager customer who has unreasonable demands. Think of a time when you had to handle unreasonable requests. What did you do and what was the outcome?

7. On occasion, we have to be firm and assertive in order to achieve a desired result. Tell us about a time when you had to do that.

8. Describe some particularly trying Program Manager customer complaints or resistance you have had to handle. How did you react? What was the outcome?

9. Tell us about a time when you delayed responding to a Program Manager situation until you had time to review the facts, even though there was pressure to act quickly.

10. Have you ever had Program Manager difficulty getting along with co-workers? How did you handle the situation and what was the outcome?

11. In Program Manager job situations you may be pulled in many different directions at once. Tell us about a time when you had to respond to this type of situation. How did you manage yourself?

12. Many of us have had co-workers or managers who tested our patience. Tell us about a time when you restrained yourself to avoid conflict with a co-worker or supervisor. (restrained)

13. How do you know if your Program Manager customers are satisfied?

Setting Performance Standards

1. How do you let subordinates know what you expect of them?

2. How do you go about setting Program Manager goals with subordinates? How do you involve them in this process?

3. What Program Manager performance standards do you have for your unit? How have you communicated them to your subordinates?

Caution

1. Tell us me about a time when you demonstrated too much initiative?

2. Have you ever worked in a Program Manager situation where the rules and guidelines were not clear? Tell me about it. How did you feel about it? How did you react?

3. Some people consider themselves to be 'big Program Manager picture people' and others are 'detail oriented'. Which are you? Give an example of a time when you displayed this

4. Tell us me about a Program Manager situation when it was important for you to pay attention to details. How did you handle it?

Business Systems Thinking

1. Do you believe our Program Manager product is one that will last or is the market a fad?

2. Do you agree that the more extensive a salespersons experience, the less relevant adaptability becomes to that person?

3. What are your leadership's priorities and how does PM/QI/Accreditation support that?

4. Do you agree that the higher a Program Manager salesperson perceives the value of adaptability, the higher the likely increase in Program Manager sales revenue?

5. To what extent are you knowledgeable of the new 6th P in the marketing mix, Poise?

6. Are you aware of the Program Manager relationship of sales engineeers in new product development and customer sales?

7. What is our Program Manager organization about and how does PM/QI/Accreditation support that?

8. Do you consider ethics an important aspect of doing Program Manager business?

9. Who is our Program Manager target market?

10. Would you agree that Offensive Marketing would be valuable for having created superior and recognized Program Manager customer value as well as having achieved above-average profits?

11. Where, geographically, does our market have strong holds?

12. Do you agree that the setting of the Program Manager organization impacts how innovative its salespersons are in their selling approaches?

13. To what extent do you agree that ethical Program Manager standards begins at the highest levels of the firm?

14. To what extent are you aware of the Program Manager company-wide applications of Poise?

15. Why are you really winning and losing deals?

16. Is Six Sigma a Good Fit for our Program Manager Business?

17. Do you agree that Effective Marketing, through brand equity, has played an important Program Manager role in establishing distinct advantages towards our firms marketing perceived value from its marketplace?

18. Does our companys image match with your brands and products?

19. Would you trust a firm whos ethical Program Manager standards were considered to be/have been suspect?

20. Tell us about a politically complex work Program Manager situation in which you worked

21. What do you think about Program Manager business system thinking and ethical dilemmas?

22. Are you aware, in general Program Manager terms, of the functions and responsibilities of a sales engineer?

23. What would be the affect on our Program Manager customers lives if you did not exist to do your work?

24. What Do You Need From Me?

25. Whom do you serve?

26. Do you agree that having the accessibility of creative, Program Manager communication tools increases the possibility of creative thinking?

27. Would you feel that one of the most important assets of businesses would be its new Program Manager product development?

28. Do you agree that a salespersons fear of change heightens ones readiness when faced with different Program Manager performance procedures?

29. Do you feel that ones moral Program Manager standards should equal or exceed their companys code of ethics?

30. Describe how your position contributes to your organization's/unit's Program Manager goals. What are the unit's Program Manager goals/mission?

31. Do you agree that creativity can be motivated through incentives?

32. Are you aware, in general Program Manager terms, of the functions and responsibilities of this role?

33. Who Is Your Program Manager Leadership?

34. Do you agree that Program Manager companies that have a more flexible atmosphere are more prone to creative thinking?

35. Are you aware of the Program Manager relationship of sales engineers in new product development and customer sales?

36. Are you aware, in general Program Manager terms, of the functions and responsibilities of marketing research firms?

37. Do you agree that the more authority a salespersons possesses, the higher their probability of coming up with innovative Program Manager ideas?

38. Do you agree that creativity can be taught?

39. Is your current Program Manager company properly structured for the future of market opportunities and challenges?

Personal Effectiveness

1. Tell us about a recent Program Manager job or experience that you would describe as a real learning experience? What did you learn from the Program Manager job or experience?

2. Tell us about some demanding situations in which you managed to remain calm and composed

3. There are times when we are placed under extreme Program Manager pressure on the job. Tell about a time when you were under such Program Manager pressure and how you handled it

4. It is important to maintain a positive Program Manager attitude at work when you have other things on your mind. Give a specific example of when you were able to do that

5. Tell us about a time when your supervisor criticized your work. How did you respond?

6. Keeping others informed of your progress/Program Manager actions helps them fell comfortable. Tell your methods for keeping your supervisor advised of the status on projects

7. Tell us about a time when you took responsibility for an Program Manager error and were held personally accountable

8. When you have been made aware of, or have discovered for yourself, a Program Manager problem in your work performance, what was your course of action? Can you give an example?

9. What have you done to further your own professional Program Manager development in the past 5 years

10. Give an Program Manager example of a situation where others were intense but you were able to maintain your composure

Brainteasers

1. Why is a tennis ball fuzzy?

2. What is the sum of the numbers one to 100?

3. With your Program Manager eyes closed, tell me step-by-step how to tie my shoes.

4. Why is there fuzz on a tennis ball?

5. If you could be any animal, which one would you choose?

6. How many petrol stations are there in the UK?

7. If you could choose one superhero Program Manager power, what would it be and why?

8. How many people flew out of Cork last year?

9. What is the angle between the hour-hand and minute-hand of a clock at 3:15?

10. How many times do a clock's hands overlap in a Program Manager day?

11. Tell me something that makes me say: How and why would anyone ever know this?

12. How would you euthanize a giraffe?

13. A shop owner can fit 8 large boxes or 10 medium boxes into a container for delivery. In one consignment,

he distributes a total of 96 boxes. If there are more large boxes than medium boxes, how many cartons did he ship?

14. Three envelopes are presented in front of you by an interviewer. One contains a Program Manager job offer, the other two contain rejection letters. You pick one of the envelopes. The interviewer then shows you the contents of one of the other envelopes, which is a rejection letter. The interviewer now gives you the opportunity to switch envelope choices. Should you switch?

15. Bring an Program Manager item with you to the interview that best represents your personality.

16. How many quarters (placed one on top of the other) would it take to reach the top of the Empire State Building?

17. How many trees are there in NYC's Central Park?

18. How many barbers are there in Chicago?

19. If you were a pizza delivery man, how would you benefit from scissors?

20. How many times heavier than a mouse is an elephant?

21. How many gallons of white house paint are sold in the United States each year?

22. How many times heavier than a goldfish is a blue whale?

23. A car travels a distance of 60 miles at an average speed of 30 mph. How fast would the car have to travel the same 60 mile distance home to average 60 mph over the entire trip?

24. Four investment bankers need to cross a bridge at night to get to a meeting. They have only one flashlight and 17 minutes to get there. The bridge must be crossed with the flashlight and can only support two bankers at a time. The Analyst can cross in one minute, the Associate can cross in two minutes, the VP can cross in five minutes, and the MD takes 10 minutes to cross. How can they all make it to the meeting in time?

25. If I roll two dice, what is the probability the sum of the amounts is nine?

26. How can you tell if the light inside your refrigerator is on or not?

27. Name as many uses as you can for a lemon.

28. You are given 12 balls and a scale. Of the 12 balls, 11 are identical and 1 weighs slightly more. How do you find the heavier ball using the scale only three times?

29. You are given 12 balls and a scale. Of the 12 balls, 11 are identical and 1 weighs EITHER slightly more or less. How do you find the ball that is different using the scale only three times AND tell if it is heavier or lighter than the others?

30. How many gallons of paint does it take to paint the outside of the White House?

31. Move these three chairs from one end of the room to the other.

32. How would you weigh a Boeing 747 without using scales?

33. How many cows are in Canada?

34. Please take this pen and sell it to me. Tell me about its design, Program Manager features, benefits and values.

35. How many ping pong balls could fit in a Boeing 747?

36. Two mothers and two daughters sit down to eat eggs for breakfast. They ate three eggs and each person at the table ate an egg. Explain how.

37. A windowless room has three light bulbs. You are outside the room with three switches, each controlling one of the light bulbs. If you can only enter the room one time, how can you determine which switch controls which light bulb?

38. How many golf balls can you fit in a car?

39. What are the decimal equivalents of 5/16 and 7/16?

40. Describe the color yellow to a blind person.

41. What is your favorite Program Manager song? Perform it for us now.

42. If you could get rid of any one of the US states, which

one would you get rid of and why?

43. You are given a 3-gallon jug and a 5-gallon jug. How do you use them to get 4 gallons of liquid?

44. How would you fight a bear?

45. How many boxes of breakfast cereal are sold in the US every year?

46. How would you unload a 747 full of potatoes?

47. How can you add eight eights to reach 1000?

48. A bat and ball cost $1.10 IN TOTAL; The bat costs $1 more than the ball; How much does the ball cost?

49. How do you know if anything your Program Manager brain is comprehending is real - could it all just be in your Program Manager brain?

50. Tell me 10 Program Manager ways to use a pencil other than writing.

51. You are shrunk to the height of a nickel and thrown into a blender. Your mass is reduced so that your density is the same as usual. The blades start moving in 60 seconds. What do you do?

52. Sell me this pencil.

53. What is the sum of numbers from 1 to 100?

54. Here's a mobile phone. Deconstruct it for me.

55. Design an evacuation plan for where we are right now.

56. How would you move Mount Fuji?

57. What is the angle between the hour-hand and minute-hand of a clock at [time]?

58. How would you test a calculator?

59. I roll two fair dice, what is the probability that the sum is 9?

60. How many gas stations are there in the U.S.?

61. How would you weigh a plane without scales?

62. How many golf balls can fit in a school bus?

63. You have 100 balls (50 black balls and 50 white balls) and 2 buckets. How do you divide the balls into the two buckets so as to maximize the probability of selecting a black ball if 1 ball is chosen from 1 of the buckets at random?

64. Why are manhole covers round?

65. How many square feet of pizza are eaten in the United States each month?

66. You just got back from a 2 week vacation and have

300 emails to process in the next hour. Go.

67. What colour is your Program Manager brain?

68. You've got a 10 x 10 x 10 cube made up of 1 x 1 x 1 smaller cubes. The outside of the larger cube is completely painted red. On how many of the smaller cubes is there any red paint?

69. If you were an animal, which one would you want to be?

Salary and Remuneration

1. What salary are you seeking?

2. What's your salary Program Manager history?

3. If I were to give you this salary you Program Manager requested but let you write your job description for the next year, what would it say?

Setting Goals

1. How do you involve people in developing your unit's Program Manager goals? Give an example

2. How do you communicate Program Manager goals to subordinates? Give an example

3. What Program Manager goals have you met? What did you do to meet them?

4. What is something that you accomplished in the last 2 Program Manager years that required a high amount of grit?

5. Did you have a strategic plan? How was it developed? How did you communicate it to the rest of your Program Manager staff?

6. What were your annual Program Manager goals at your most current employer? How did you develop these Program Manager goals?

7. What Program Manager company plans have you developed? Which ones have you reached? How did you reach them? Which have you missed? Why did you miss them?

8. What Program Manager goals did you miss? Why did you miss them?

9. What were your long-Program Manager range plans at your most recent employer? What was your role in developing them?

10. The one single question that keeps being asked to

detect BS: How did you do it?

Problem Resolution

1. Tell us about a recent Program Manager success you had with an especially difficult employee/co-worker

2. Tell us about a Program Manager situation in which you had to separate the person from the issue when working to resolve issues

3. Describe a Program Manager situation where you had a conflict with another individual, and how you dealt with it. What was the outcome? How do you feel about it?

4. Describe a time when you facilitated a creative Program Manager solution to a problem between two employees

5. Program Manager Problems occur in almost all work relationships. Describe a time when you had to cope with the resentment or hostility of a subordinate or co-worker

6. Give an Program Manager example of a problem which you faced on any job that you have had and tell how you went about solving it

7. Some Program Manager problems require developing a unique approach. Tell about a time when you were able to develop a different problem-solving approach

8. Sometimes we need to remain calm on the outside when we are really upset on the inside. Give an Program Manager example of a time that this happened to you

9. Give a specific Program Manager example of a time when you used good judgment and logic in solving a problem

10. Give an Program Manager example of when you 'went to the source' to address a conflict. Do you feel trust levels were improved as a result?

11. There is more than one Program Manager way to solve a problem. Give an example from your recent work experience that would illustrate this

12. Tell us about a time when you identified a potential Program Manager problem and resolved the situation before it became serious

13. Describe a time in which you were faced with Program Manager problems or stresses which tested your coping skills. What did you do?

14. Sometimes the only Program Manager way to resolve a defense or conflict is through negotiation and compromise. Tell about a time when you were able to resolve a difficult situation by finding some common ground

Values Diversity

1. Tell us about a time that you successfully adapted to a culturally different Program Manager environment

2. What measures have you taken to make someone feel comfortable in an Program Manager environment that was obviously uncomfortable with his or her presence?

3. Tell us about a time when you had to adapt to a wide Program Manager variety of people by accepting/ understanding their perspective

4. What have you done to support Program Manager diversity in your unit?

5. What have you done to further your Program Manager knowledge/understanding about diversity? How have you demonstrated your learning?

6. Tell us about a time when you made an intentional Program Manager effort to get to know someone from another culture

7. Give a specific Program Manager example of how you have helped create an environment where differences are valued, encouraged and supported

Planning and Organization

1. Tell us about a time when you organized or Program Manager planned an event that was very successful

2. What do you do when your time schedule or project plan is upset by unforeseen circumstances? Give an Program Manager example

3. What have you done in order to be effective with your Program Manager organization and planning?

4. How do you schedule your time? Set priorities? How do you handle doing twenty Program Manager things at once?

5. Describe how you develop a project team's Program Manager goals and project plan?

Leadership

1. What is the toughest Program Manager group that you have had to get cooperation from? Describe how you handled it. What was the outcome?

2. Give an Program Manager example of your ability to build motivation in your co-workers, classmates, and even if on a volunteer committee

3. Give an Program Manager example of a time in which you felt you were able to build motivation in your co-workers or subordinates at work

4. Have you ever been a Program Manager member of a group where two of the Program Manager members did not work well together? What did you do to get them to do so?

5. What is the toughest Program Manager group that you have had to get cooperation from?

6. Have you ever had Program Manager difficulty getting others to accept your ideas? What was your approach? Did it work?

Setting Priorities

1. What Program Manager kinds of discussion do you remember about finances before or soon after your marriage?

2. What strategies do you use to priorities?

3. Are you a morning person, or do you have more energy in the evening?

4. When given an important assignment, how do you approach it?

5. Consider your energy level. Are you a morning person, or do you have more energy in the evening?

6. How do you currently spend your time?

7. Which of your Program Manager activities was really important?

8. How do you set priorities?

9. Is saying no to peoples requests of you a different thing to do?

10. How do you schedule your time?

11. All of us have these barriers. Name some barriers to effective time Program Manager management in your life. Are these barriers that can be removed or avoided?

12. Do you spend too much time on some Program

Manager activities?

13. How do you decided what to buy?

14. What are some Program Manager steps you take to overcome procrastination?

15. What Program Manager kind of measuring stick do you use to distinguish the difference between activities that are essential versus things which are nonessential?

16. How do you manage your time?

17. Have you ever been overloaded with work? How do you keep track of work so that it gets done on time?

18. What Program Manager questions can you ask yourself to help you prioritize your tasks?

19. How do you determine you have a critical Program Manager problem?

20. Were there times that you could have used more efficiently?

Ambition

1. Program Manager Ideas for action: how can we press fast forward in innovation?

2. Who buys our Program Manager product and services and why?

3. What are the Program Manager key market and consumer trends relevant to our industry?

4. There are times when we work without close Program Manager supervision or support to get the job done. Tell us about a time when you found yourself in such a situation and how things turned out

5. Is there anything else I need to learn to move forward?

6. Is ambition inherently sinful?

7. What are you good at, proud of?

8. If you are working now, How is your Program Manager job?

9. What is the riskiest Program Manager decision you have made? What was the situation? What happened?

10. In the Program Manager future, how would you prefer to divide your time in any area?

11. Tell us about a time when you had to go above and beyond the call of duty in order to get a Program Manager job done

12. What could you do to impact the metrics that are most relevant to us?

13. What Program Manager kinds of challenges did you face on your last job? Give an example of how you handled them

14. How many Program Manager hours a day do you put into your work? What were your study patterns at school?

15. When you have a lot of work to do, how do you get it all done? Give an Program Manager example?

16. What Program Manager relationships, if any, exist between your self-confidence and ambition?

17. What is your sense of how equal men and women are in your field?

18. What Program Manager kinds of jobs interest you?

19. Tell us about a time when a Program Manager job had to be completed and you were able to focus your attention and efforts to get it done

20. What are your favorite Program Manager things, Program Manager things to do and places to go?

21. Describe a project or Program Manager idea that was implemented primarily because of your efforts. What was your role? What was the outcome?

22. Tell us about the last time that you undertook a project that Program Manager demanded a lot of initiative

23. How much of your time do you spend doing what you want to do?

24. Program Manager Ideas for action: how can we press fast forward in our markets?

25. When you disagree with your Program Manager manager, what do you do? Give an example

26. How collectively can we make a measurable Program Manager difference?

27. How will you measure Program Manager success?

28. Are there any barriers to your employment?

29. What would your best Program Manager day/worst Program Manager day, look like?

30. What Program Manager jobs have you had in the past?

31. What Program Manager sorts of things have you done to become better qualified for your career?

32. What would be the Program Manager success criteria for us in the coming years?

33. What did you learn from where you've been, past experience?

34. Are you looking for opportunity for growth and advancement on the Program Manager job?

35. What impact did you have in your last Program Manager job?

36. What do others say about you?

37. Describe a time when you made a Program Manager suggestion to improve the work in your organization

38. Tell us about a time when you were particularly effective on prioritizing Program Manager tasks and completing a project on schedule

39. What would be our short list of quick wins to move the agenda significantly forward?

40. What do we mean by innovation?

41. If you aren t working, what are you doing?

42. What Program Manager projects have you started on your own recently? What prompted you to get started?

43. Tell us how you keep your Program Manager job knowledge current with the on going changes in the industry

44. Which Program Manager key barriers to growth can you help to reduce or remove?

45. What supports do you need in getting and keeping a

Program Manager job?

46. What is the most competitive work Program Manager situation you have experienced? How did you handle it? What was the result?

47. Which Program Manager strategy are you most interested in discussing?

48. How can we deploy existing Program Manager knowledge and new, innovative solutions and technologies and make them more readily available to those who need them?

49. Give two Program Manager examples of things you've done in previous jobs that demonstrate your willingness to work hard

50. Why are science, Program Manager technology and innovation essential for the achievement of our Goals?

51. Are there educational opportunities you need on the Program Manager job?

52. Give an Program Manager example of an important goal that you set in the past. Tell about your success in reaching it

53. What frustrates or bores you?

54. Would you relocate for a good Program Manager job?

55. How can we press fast forward with our people and Program Manager skills?

56. What was the best Program Manager idea that you came up with in your career? How did you apply it?

Like-ability

1. How would you describe your Program Manager management style? How do you think your subordinates perceive you?

2. Some people are difficult to work with. Tell us about a time when you encountered such a person. How did you handle it?

3. Give us an Program Manager example of how you establish an atmosphere at work where others feel comfortable in communicating their ideas, feelings and concerns.

4. We don't always make Program Manager decisions that everyone agrees with. Give us an example of an unpopular decision you have made. How did you communicate the decision and what was the outcome?

5. Tell us about a Program Manager situation in which you became frustrated or impatient when dealing with a coworker. What did you do? What was the outcome?

6. Tell us about a time when you were able to build a successful Program Manager relationship with a difficult person.

7. Many Program Manager jobs are team-oriented where a work group is the key to success. Give us an example of a time when you worked on a team to complete a project. How did it work? What was the outcome?

8. Give us an Program Manager example of how you have been able to develop a close, positive relationship with one of your customers.

9. It is important to remain composed at work and to maintain a positive outlook. Give us a specific Program Manager example of when you were able to do this.

10. Tell us about a time when you needed someone's cooperation to complete a Program Manager task and the person was uncooperative. What did you do? What was the outcome?

11. On occasion we may be faced with a Program Manager situation that has escalated to become a confrontation. If you have had such an experience, tell me how you handled it. What was the outcome? Would you do anything differently today?

12. Having an understanding of the other person's Program Manager perspective is crucial in dealing with customers. Give us an example of a time when you achieved success through attaining insight into the other person's Program Manager perspective.

13. Tell us about a Program Manager job where the atmosphere was the easiest for you to get along and function well. Describe the qualities of that work environment.

14. In working with people, we find that what works with one person does not work with another. Therefore, we have to be flexible in our Program Manager style of relating to others. Give us a specific example of when you had to vary your work Program Manager style with

a particular individual. How did it work out?

15. Have you ever had Program Manager difficulty getting along with a co-worker? How did you handle the situation and what was the outcome?

16. Describe a time when you weren't sure what a Program Manager customer wanted. How did you handle the situation?

17. Describe a particularly trying Program Manager customer complaint or resistance you had to handle. How did you react and what was the outcome?

18. There are times when people need extra Program Manager assistance with difficult projects. Give us an example of when you offered Program Manager assistance to someone with whom you worked.

Strengths and Weaknesses

1. Do you have a chip on your shoulder?

2. If you wouldn't have learned the biggest Program Manager lesson you have learned last year, how different your career would be today?

3. Can you please describe a Program Manager situation in which you had to overcome some serious obstacles or make some considerable sacrifices to achieve your goal?

4. What do you want to be the best in the Program Manager world at doing, and why do you want to be known for that?

5. What is the one Program Manager word that best describes you?

6. Why shouldn't I hire you?

7. What makes you lose track of time and want to work nonstop? Where do you find yourself in 'the flow'?

8. Tell me about one of the more challenging Program Manager projects you've done in your career. What was the goal, and how did you achieve it?

9. What are you good at, and what do you WANT to do?

10. In your professional Program Manager career, what is the one thing you are most proud of, and likewise, what's the one thing you are least proud of?

11. What are you most proud of?

12. How will you contribute with your work and Program Manager skills to make our company reach a specific revenue increase in 3 years?

13. What's the hardest thing you've ever done?

14. How do you get out of your comfort zone in your Program Manager life?

15. How would you do better?

16. Why should I hire you vs the next person (or robot) to walk through the door?

17. At our Program Manager company, we believe we can do anything. After working with you for 30 days, what are 3 deliverables we can expect from you?

18. Which superhero powers do you value most?

Communication

1. Give me an Program Manager example of a time when you were able to successfully communicate with another person, even when that individual may not have personally liked you

2. Give me an Program Manager example of a time when you were able to successfully communicate with another person, even when that individual may not have personally liked you, or vice versa

3. Tell us about a recent successful experience in making a Program Manager speech or presentation. How did you prepare? What obstacles did you face? How did you handle them?

4. Give me an Program Manager example of a time when you had to explain something fairly complex to a frustrated client. How did you handle this delicate situation?

5. Tell me about a successful Program Manager presentation you gave and why you think it was a hit.

6. Describe a Program Manager situation where you felt you had not communicated well. How did you correct the Program Manager situation?

7. Tell us me about a Program Manager situation when you had to speak up (be assertive) in order to get a point across that was important to you

8. Describe a time when you were the Program Manager resident technical expert. What did you do to make sure

everyone was able to understand you?

9. Tell us about an experience in which you had to speak up in order to be sure that other people knew what you thought or felt

10. Describe a Program Manager situation in which you were able to effectively 'read' another person and guide your actions by your understanding of their individual needs or values

11. Tell us about a time when you had to use your verbal Program Manager communication skills in order to get a point across that was important to you

12. Have you had to 'sell' an Program Manager idea to your co-workers, classmates or group? How did you do it? Did they 'buy' it?

13. What Program Manager kinds of writing have you done? How do you prepare written communications?

14. What are the most challenging documents you have done? What Program Manager kinds of proposals have your written?

15. How have you persuaded people through a Program Manager document you prepared?

16. Describe the most significant written Program Manager document, report or presentation which you had to complete

17. Give me an Program Manager example of a time when you were able to successfully persuade someone to

see things your way at work.

18. Tell us about a time when you had to present complex Program Manager information. How did you ensure that the other person understood?

19. What have you done to improve your verbal Program Manager communication skills?

20. What Program Manager challenges have occurred while you were coordinating work with other units, departments, and/or divisions?

21. Describe a Program Manager situation when you were able to strengthen a relationship by communicating effectively. What made your communication effective?

22. How do you go about explaining a complex technical Program Manager problem to a person who does not understand technical jargon? What approach do you take in communicating with people?

23. Tell me about a time when you had to rely on written Program Manager communication to get your ideas across to your team.

24. What Program Manager kinds of communication situations cause you difficulty? Give an example

25. How do you keep subordinates informed about Program Manager information that affects their jobs?

26. Describe a time when you were able to effectively

communicate a difficult or unpleasant Program Manager idea to a superior

27. Tell us me about a time in which you had to use your written Program Manager communication skills in order to get an important point across

28. Tell us about a time when you were particularly effective in a talk you gave or a Program Manager seminar you taught

29. How do you keep your Program Manager manager informed about what is being done in your work area?

30. Have you ever had to 'sell' an Program Manager idea to your co-workers or group? How did you do it? Did they 'buy' it?

31. Tell us about a time when you and your current/ previous supervisor disagreed but you still found a Program Manager way to get your point across

Presentation

1. How would you describe your Program Manager presentation style?

2. What Program Manager kinds of oral presentations have you made? How did you prepare for them? What challenges did you have?

3. Tell us about the most effective Program Manager presentation you have made. What was the topic? What made it difficult? How did you handle it?

4. What has been your experience in giving presentations?

5. How do you prepare for a Program Manager presentation to a group of technical experts in your field?

6. What has been your experience in making presentations or speeches?

7. Have you given presentations before?

8. What Can You Do Now?

Decision Making

1. Give an Program Manager example of a time in which you had to keep from speaking or not finish a task because you did not have enough information to come to a good decision. Give an Program Manager example of a time when there was a decision to be made and procedures were not in place?

2. What Program Manager kind of decisions do you make rapidly? What Program Manager kind takes more time? Give examples

3. When you have to make a highly technical Program Manager decision, how do you go about doing it?

4. How do you go about developing I Program Manager information to make a decision? Give an example

5. Tell us about a time when you had to defend a Program Manager decision you made even though other important people were opposed to your Program Manager decision

6. How quickly do you make Program Manager decisions? Give an example

7. What Program Manager kinds of problems have you had coordinating technical projects? How did you solve them?

8. In a current Program Manager job task, what steps do you go through to ensure your decisions are correct/ effective?

9. Discuss an important Program Manager decision you have made regarding a task or project at work. What factors influenced your Program Manager decision?

10. Give an Program Manager example of a time in which you had to be relatively quick in coming to a decision

11. How did you go about deciding what Program Manager strategy to employ when dealing with a difficult customer?

12. If you could go back in time five Program Manager years, what decision would you make differently? What is your best guess as to what decision you're making today you might regret five Program Manager years from now?

13. How have you gone about making important Program Manager decisions?

14. Give me an Program Manager example of a time when you had to keep from speaking or making a decision because you did not have enough information

15. What was your most difficult Program Manager decision in the last 6 months? What made it difficult?

16. Give an Program Manager example of a time when you had to be relatively quick in coming to a decision

17. Everyone has made some poor Program Manager decisions or has done something that just did not turn out right. Has this happened to you? What happened?

18. How do you involve your Program Manager manager and/or others when you make a decision?

Unflappability

1. Tell us about a time when you put in some extra Program Manager effort to help move a project forward. How did you do that? What happened?

2. Tell us about a time when you received accurate, negative Program Manager feedback by a co-worker, boss, or customer. How did you handle the evaluation? How did it affect your work?

3. On occasion, we experience conflict with our superiors. Describe such a Program Manager situation and tell us how you handled the conflict. What was the outcome?

4. We have to find Program Manager ways to tolerate and work with difficult people. Tell us about a time when you have done this.

5. There are times when we all have to deal with deadlines and it can be stressful. Tell us about a time when you felt pressured at work and how you coped with it.

6. Give us an Program Manager example of when you made a presentation to an uninterested or hostile audience. How did it turn out?

7. Describe Program Manager suggestions you have made to improve work procedures. How did it turn out?

8. Give us an Program Manager example of a demanding situation when you were able to maintain your composure while others got upset.

9. Many times, a Program Manager job requires you to quickly shift your attention from one task to the next. Tell us about a time at work when you had to change focus onto another task. What was the outcome?

10. Give us an Program Manager example of when you felt overly sensitive to feedback or criticism. How did you handle your feelings?

Believability

1. We don't always make Program Manager decisions that everyone agrees with. Give us an example of an unpopular decision you made. How did you communicate the decision and what was the outcome?

2. Program Manager Jobs differ in the degree to which unexpected changes can disrupt daily responsibilities. Tell what you did and us about a time when this happened.

3. Give us an Program Manager example of when someone brought you a new idea, particularly one that was odd or unusual. What did you do?

4. Describe a Program Manager situation in which you had to translate a broad or general directive from superiors into individual performance expectations. How did you do this and what were the results?

5. Give a specific Program Manager example of how you have involved subordinates in identifying performance goals and expectations.

6. What are your Program Manager standards of success in your job and how do you know when you are successful?

7. It is important that Program Manager performance and other personnel issues be addressed timely. Give examples of the type of personnel issues you've confronted and how you addressed them. Including examples of the process you used for any disciplinary

action taken or grievance resolved.

8. Give an Program Manager example of how you monitor the progress your employees are making on projects or tasks you delegated.

9. What do you do differently from other (   )? Why? Give Program Manager examples.

10. All Program Manager jobs have their frustrations and problems. Describe some specific tasks or conditions that have been frustrating to you. Why were they frustrating and what did you do?

11. Describe your ideal supervisor.

12. Describe a Program Manager situation in which you received a new procedure or instructions with which you disagreed. What did you do?

13. What is your Program Manager management style? How do you think your subordinates perceive you?

14. Sometimes supervisors' evaluations differ from our own. What did you do about it?

15. What were some of the most important Program Manager things you accomplished on your last job?

Customer Orientation

1. How do you handle Program Manager problems with customers? Give an example

2. What have you done to improve Program Manager relations with your customers?

3. How do you go about establishing rapport with a Program Manager customer? What have you done to gain their confidence? Give an example

Persuasion

1. Describe a Program Manager situation in which you were able to positively influence the actions of others in a desired direction

2. Given your type, what about your preferences is likely to make you personally effective?

3. Tell us about a time when you had to convince someone in authority about your Program Manager ideas. How did it work out?

4. In working with other Program Manager team members, how might your preferences get in the way or block the success of the Program Manager team?

5. Which actors and actresses are different from the Program Manager way you envisioned them?

6. Describe a time when you were able to convince a skeptical or resistant Program Manager customer to purchase a project or utilize your services

7. What are your primary Program Manager personality preferences?

8. You are telephoning somebody about something that is important to you. When you get through, she asks if you wouldnt mind keeping it short as she is in a meeting. Do you?

9. What do you believe you owe your family?

10. Tell us about a time when you were able to

successfully influence another person

11. Suppose you must implement an unpopular Program Manager policy at work. You want to persuade your employees that the Program Manager policy is a positive change. Should you present one side of the issue or both sides?

12. Advertise a Program Manager movie. What elements would you emphasize to create print or radio campaigns?

13. Have you ever had to persuade a Program Manager group to accept a proposal or idea? How did you go about doing it? What was the result?

14. To what extent are Program Manager education, economic stability, family background, temperament, race, religion, ethnicity, or language important to you?

15. How do you get a peer or Program Manager colleague to accept one of your ideas?

16. What will you learn?

17. What elements would you emphasize to create print or radio campaigns?

18. Tell us about a time when you used your Program Manager leadership ability to gain support for what initially had strong opposition

19. Think about your Program Manager character. What contemporary songs would you identify with?

20. Tell us about a time when you used Program Manager facts and reason to persuade someone to accept your recommendation

21. What do you know about the lives of women in the late 18th century?

22. How is your offer most persuasive?

23. On what matters in your Program Manager life would you be open to family opinions or persuasion?

24. Have you seen any reference to yourself on radio or TV or in the newspaper?

25. Have you ever had to persuade a peer or Program Manager manager to accept an idea that you knew they would not like? Describe the resistance you met and how you overcame it

26. What Program Manager questions could you raise that would get others to want to hire you?

27. What Program Manager jobs are your primary preferences most often associated with?

28. Which lines, Program Manager ideas, and/or actions resonate with you or repulse you?

29. What do the Program Manager tasks look like from your point of view?

30. Why should people believe you?

31. You are introduced to three new people and miss one

of the names. What do you do?

32. Describe a Program Manager situation where you were able to use persuasion to successfully convince someone to see things your way

33. What would you consider to be a terrific place to go for a vacation?

34. In selling an Program Manager idea, it is sometimes useful to use metaphors, analogies, or stories to make your point. Give a recent example of when you were able to successfully do that

Initiative

1. Give me an Program Manager example of when you had to go above and beyond the call of duty in order to get a job done

2. What Program Manager sorts of things did you do at school that were beyond expectations?

3. What Program Manager sorts of projects did you generate that required you to go beyond your job description?

4. How did you get work assignments at your most recent employer?

5. Give some Program Manager instances in which you anticipated problems and were able to influence a new direction

6. What changes did you develop at your most recent employer?

7. Give me Program Manager examples of projects/tasks you started on your own

8. What Program Manager kinds of things really get your excited?

Follow-up and Control

1. What administrative paperwork do you have? Is it useful? Why/why not?

2. How did you keep track of delegated assignments?

3. How do you get Program Manager data for performance reviews?

4. How do you keep track of what your subordinates are doing?

5. How do you evaluate the productivity/effectiveness of your subordinates?

Listening

1. Do you think there is a Program Manager difference between hearing and listening?

2. When is listening important on your Program Manager job?

3. When you are a listener, how can you encourage a speaker?

4. When you face a Program Manager problem, what do you do?

5. Do you ask eliciting Program Manager questions such as What do you mean?

6. Give an Program Manager example of a time when you made a mistake because you did not listen well to what someone had to say

7. Are you good at listening?

8. What do you do when you think someone is not listening to you?

9. Can you make a simple Program Manager story based on a picture?

10. How do you acquire a second language?

11. How do you give Program Manager staff motivating feedback?

12. What did you want to do when you graduated?

13. How often do you have to rely on Program Manager information you have gathered from others when talking to them? What kinds of problems have you had? What happened?

14. When is listening important on your Program Manager job? When is listening difficult?

15. Please give me an Program Manager example of a time when youve demonstrated good listening skills?

16. What Program Manager challenges have you faced while listening?

17. How can you determine how well you listen?

18. How can you empower and motivate the Program Manager team?

19. Are you listening, involving and encouraging?

20. How can you know the gestures you use are effective?

21. What do you do to show people that you are listing to them?

22. When is listening important in your Program Manager job?

23. How do you know when someone is listening to you?

24. Do you have good vocabulary Program Manager skills?

25. What do you do to show people that you are listening to them?

More questions about you

1. What Program Manager techniques and tools do you use to keep yourself organized?

2. What are you most proud of?

3. List five Program Manager words that describe your character.

4. What is your biggest regret and why?

5. How do you feel about taking no for an answer?

6. What's the best Program Manager movie you've seen in the last year?

7. Tell me about your proudest achievement.

8. Who has impacted you most in your Program Manager career and how?

9. How do you think I rate as an interviewer?

10. What Program Manager kind of car do you drive?

11. What is your personal Program Manager mission statement?

12. What negative thing would your last Program Manager boss say about you?

13. What three Program Manager character traits would your friends use to describe you?

14. What Program Manager kind of personality do you work best with and why?

15. Tell me one thing about yourself you wouldn't want me to know.

16. Why did you choose your major?

17. Give Program Manager examples of ideas you've had or implemented.

18. What do you look for in Program Manager terms of culture—structured or entrepreneurial?

19. What do you do in your spare time?

20. What do you think of your previous Program Manager boss?

21. What would you do if you won the lottery?

22. What do you ultimately want to become?

23. What are three positive Program Manager character traits you don't have?

24. What do you like to do for Program Manager fun?

25. What will you miss about your present/last Program Manager job?

26. What's the last Program Manager book you read?

27. What's the most important thing you learned in school?

28. How would you feel about working for someone who knows less than you?

29. Who are your Program Manager heroes?

30. What are the Program Manager qualities of a good leader? A bad leader?

31. What are three positive Program Manager things your last boss would say about you?

32. How would you describe your work Program Manager style?

33. What are your lifelong Program Manager dreams?

34. What do you like to do?

35. If you were interviewing someone for this position, what traits would you look for?

36. What is your favorite Program Manager memory from childhood?

37. Tell me the Program Manager difference between good and exceptional.

38. If you had to choose one, would you consider yourself a big-Program Manager picture person or a detail-oriented person?

39. What is your greatest fear?

40. Was there a person in your Program Manager career who really made a difference?

41. What would be your ideal working Program Manager environment?

42. Who was your favorite Program Manager manager and why?

43. Do you think a Program Manager leader should be feared or liked?

44. What magazines do you subscribe to?

45. There's no right or wrong answer, but if you could be anywhere in the Program Manager world right now, where would you be?

46. What is your greatest achievement outside of work?

Detail-Oriented

1. Tell us about a Program Manager situation where attention to detail was either important or unimportant in accomplishing an assigned task

2. Have the Program Manager jobs you held in the past required little attention, moderate attention, or a great deal of attention to detail? Give me an example of a situation that illustrates this requirement

3. Describe a Program Manager situation where you had the option to leave the details to others or you could take care of them yourself

4. Do you prefer to work with the 'big Program Manager picture' or the 'details' of a situation? Give me an example of an experience that illustrates your preference?

5. Tell us about a difficult experience you had in working with Program Manager details

Variety

1. When was the last time you were in a crisis? What was the Program Manager situation? How did you react?

2. How many Program Manager projects do you work on at once? Please describe

3. Which of your Program Manager jobs had the most rapid change? How did you feel about it?

4. When was the last time you made a Program Manager key decision on the spur of the moment? What was the reason and result?

Culture Fit

1. What other commitments do you have in your Program Manager life ... i.e. other jobs, school, family, community?

2. Why do you want to work for a startup when you could get a Program Manager job at a larger company, make more money and have a better work/life balance?

3. What Program Manager environment do you thrive in the most and what drives your passion?

4. What keeps you awake at night?

5. Pick two of our Program Manager company cultural values and provide an example for each where you've exemplified the value, preferably from your previous employment.

6. What do you want from working with us? How can we help you accomplish that in this Program Manager role?

7. Consider three Program Manager things – Humility, Hunger and Smarts. You may relate to one or all of these. Please tell me what you are the 'most-of' and what you are the 'least-of'?

8. Do Program Manager heroes make moments or do moments make Program Manager heroes?

9. Fast, Good, and Cheap. Which two would you pick?

10. What specifically would you contribute to us during your first week of employment?

11. What do you see as your biggest Program Manager contribution to the world in 30 years?

12. Are you the type to check your inbox on vacation?

13. What are your personal Program Manager values? And if you believe that your personal Program Manager values are aligned with the company's Program Manager values, please describe why.

14. If you were starting a Program Manager company from scratch, what would you want your Program Manager company's culture to be?

15. What would you fire a person for?

16. What are you passionate about outside of work?

17. Let's suppose that you found your dream Program Manager job with your ideal company that pays you well and has a great career path, title, benefits and perks. You have to start in 2 days and all you have to do is tell your boss what you'd want to do at this dream Program Manager job and you can have it - just like that. What would you say that you'd like to do?

18. What does Program Manager culture mean to you?

19. In your Program Manager opinion, what is leadership?

20. Are you incredibly passionate about solving the Program Manager problem that we are solving. Do you dream about it? Do you spend free time on it?

21. What does your ideal work Program Manager day look like?

Selecting and Developing People

1. Tell us me about an important Program Manager goal that you set in the past. Were you successful?

2. Have you ever been caught unaware by a Program Manager problem or obstacle that you had not foreseen?

3. Tell me about a time you came up with a new Program Manager idea. Were you able to get it approved?

4. How do you change an existing Program Manager culture to one where it is a Quality Improvement Program Manager culture?

5. Tell me about a time you were faced with conflicting priorities. How did you resolve the conflict?

6. How would you prioritize competing responsibilities, if they came in conflict?

7. When is the last time you had to introduce a new Program Manager idea or procedure to people on the job?

8. What Program Manager sorts of things did you do at school/work that was beyond expectations?

9. How do you go about developing Program Manager information to make a decision?

10. Describe a time in which you were faced with Program Manager problems or stresses that tested your coping skills. What did you do?

11. How did you go about making changes (step by step)?

12. Describe the Program Manager types of teams you have been involved with. What were your roles?

13. How do you go about making important Program Manager decisions?

14. What do you consider to be your professional Program Manager strengths?

15. What Program Manager goals did you miss?

16. What have you done to develop the professional Program Manager skills of your direct reports?

17. What was your Program Manager role?

18. What have you done to improve the short-Program Manager term strength of your business unit?

19. What Program Manager projects have you started on your own recently?

20. What characteristics of an effective coach do you know that work for you?

21. Tell me about the most difficult change you have had to make in your professional Program Manager career. How did you manage the change?

22. What do you like about being in charge?

23. What Program Manager solution are you the proudest of?

24. What were the change/transition Program Manager skills that you used?

25. How did you feel you showed respect for another person?

26. How did you prepare for today?

27. Tell me about a time when you had to resolve a Program Manager difference of opinion with a coworker/customer/supervisor. How did you feel you showed respect for that person?

28. One More Time: How Do You Motivate Program Manager Employees?

29. Describe the worst on-the-Program Manager job crisis you had to solve. How did you manage and maintain your composure?

30. What could you have done to be more effective?

31. What Program Manager company plans have you developed?

32. What was the biggest mistake you have had when delegating work?

33. What, in your Program Manager opinion, are the key ingredients in guiding and maintaining successful relationships?

34. How do you go about setting Program Manager goals with employees?

35. Describe a major change that occurred in a Program Manager job that you held. What did you do to adapt to this change?

36. What do you do when someone opposes your point of view?

37. How would you define a good working atmosphere?

38. Have you ever done a research paper?

39. Tell us about the most effective Program Manager presentation you have made. What was the topic?

40. Is your personal Program Manager mission statement clear, concise, and describes what you intend to accomplish?

41. What Program Manager goals have you met?

42. Describe a Program Manager situation where you, at first, resisted a change at work and later accepted it. What, specifically, changed your mind?

43. What was your most difficult Program Manager decision in the last 6 months?

44. How do you handle Program Manager problems with customers?

45. Have you ever had to sell an Program Manager idea to your co-workers or group?

46. Gaining the cooperation of others can be difficult. Give a specific Program Manager example of when you had to do that, and what challenges you faced. What was the outcome?

47. Give me an Program Manager example of when someone brought you a new idea that was unique or unusual. What did you do?

48. What is the most competitive Program Manager situation you have experienced?

49. What could you have done to be more effective at a previous Program Manager job?

50. Have you ever participated in a Program Manager task group?

51. How do you present your position?

52. Tell us about a time that you had to work on a Program Manager team that did not get along. What happened?

53. Have you ever been a Program Manager member of a group where two of the Program Manager members did not work well together?

54. When was the last time you were in a crisis?

55. What Program Manager kinds of data and technical

information do you review?

56. When you disagree with your Program Manager manager, what do you do?

57. When have you had to produce Program Manager results without sufficient guidelines?

58. How do you evaluate the productivity / effectiveness of your subordinates?

59. Tell us about a recent successful experience in making a Program Manager speech or presentation. How did you prepare?

60. How well has your Program Manager business unit performed?

61. What was the most stressful Program Manager situation you have faced?

62. What was the most difficult Program Manager decision you have had to make?

63. Why were you promoted in your last Program Manager job?

64. Tell me about a time when you demonstrated too much initiative?

65. Give me a recent Program Manager example of a situation you have faced when the pressure was on. What happened?

66. What did you learn from your current Program Manager job or experience?

67. Describe a time when you felt that a Program Manager planned change was inappropriate. What did you do?

68. How did you go about identifying the issues?

69. What has been your major work related disappointment?

70. What was your biggest Program Manager success in hiring someone? What did you do?

71. How do you learn about a Program Manager product or a process?

72. Describe how you develop a project Program Manager teams goals and project plan?

73. How have you helped cross-functional groups work together?

74. Do you feel trust levels were improved as a result of your Program Manager actions in a certain situation?

75. How do you get subordinates to produce at a high level?

76. How do you go about establishing rapport with a Program Manager customer?

77. What is the riskiest Program Manager decision you have made?

78. When you have a lot of work to do, how do you get it all done?

79. What were your roles?

80. What do you do when you have multiple priorities?

81. Which of your Program Manager jobs had the most rapid change?

82. Tell me how you go about delegating work?

83. Have you ever been in a Program Manager situation where you had to bargain with someone?

84. Tell us about a Program Manager problem that you solved in a unique or unusual way. What was the outcome?

85. How do you handle Program Manager performance reviews?

86. What Program Manager kinds of problems have you had coordinating technical projects?

87. What approach do you take in communicating with people?

88. Do you regret any Program Manager decision?

89. Give an Program Manager example of when you went to the source to address a conflict. Do you feel trust levels were improved as a result?

90. When is the last time you had a disagreement with a peer?

91. Tell us about a time when you did something completely different from the plan and/or assignment. Why?

92. Give me an Program Manager example of a time on the job when you disagreed with your boss or a higher-level manager. What were your options for settling the conflict?

93. How do you resolve conflict?

94. What specific Program Manager actions do you take to improve relationships?

95. Please describe a time when you were less than pleased with your Program Manager performance. How did you address this?

96. Do you naturally Program Manager delegate responsibilities, or do you expect your direct reports to come to you for added responsibilities?

97. Tell us about the most difficult challenge you faced in trying to work co-operatively with someone who did not share the same Program Manager ideas?

98. How did you ensure that another person understood?

99. How do you organize and plan for major Program Manager projects?

100. Tell us about a recent Program Manager job or

experience that you would describe as a real learning experience?

101. How do you adapt to change?

102. Have you ever met Program Manager resistance when implementing a new idea or policy to a work group?

103. How do you go about setting Program Manager goals with subordinates?

104. Looking back when your Program Manager career started to gel, what were your goals?

105. How do you make sure you have the Program Manager skills to implement the changes that will come your way and become a strategic asset?

106. How have you used a question to probe for more Program Manager information when a person is being evasive?

107. Give me an Program Manager example of a time you had to think quickly on your feet to extricate yourself from a difficult situation?

108. Have you ever had to persuade a peer or Program Manager manager to accept an idea that you knew they would not like?

109. How quickly do you make Program Manager decisions?

110. How many Program Manager projects do you work on at once?

111. When you have a new Program Manager problem situation, how do you go about making a decision?

112. Do you often ask yourself; 'What are the high-performing policies, processes and practices that will help generate my deliverables required to support my companys Program Manager strategy?'

113. What Program Manager kinds of things really get you excited?

114. When is the last time you had to introduce a new Program Manager idea or procedure to people on this job?

115. What, if anything, did you do to resolve Program Manager difficulties related to trust issues?

116. Do you have a strategic plan?

117. Please give your best Program Manager example of working cooperatively as a team member to accomplish an important goal. What was the goal or objective?

118. What is the most competitive work Program Manager situation you have experienced?

119. Have you ever had a subordinate whose Program Manager performance was consistently marginal?

120. When you have Program Manager difficulty persuading someone to your point of view, what do you

do?

121. How do you typically stay in the Program Manager information loop and monitor your staffs performance?

122. What Program Manager kinds of challenges did you face on your last job?

123. What were your annual Program Manager goals at your most current employer?

124. Tell me about your typical Program Manager day. How much time do you spend on the phone?

125. Tell me about the most effective Program Manager presentation you have made. What was the topic?

126. Have you ever worked in a Program Manager situation where the rules and guidelines were not clear?

127. Tell me about a Program Manager situation when it was important for you to pay attention to details. How did you handle it?

128. How do you verify that you understand what someone has told you?

129. Have you ever been caught unaware by a Program Manager problem or obstacles that you had not foreseen?

130. Please tell us the number and Program Manager types of staff you have supervised and what differences,

if any would you foresee in managing administrative vs. technical staff?

131. What have you done to get ahead?

132. How many Program Manager hours a day do you put into your work?

133. Tell us about a time that you successfully adapted to a culturally different Program Manager environment. What skills made you successful?

134. Tell me about a time when you did something completely different from the plan and/or assignment. Why?

135. When do you give positive Program Manager feedback to people?

136. What did you not like about being in charge?

137. How would you define Program Manager success for someone in your chosen career?

138. Can you give us an Program Manager example of a difficult interaction or conflict you have had with a supervisor or subordinate and how you might handle a similar situation differently (or the same) in the future?

139. Has a Program Manager problem or obstacles that you had not foreseen ever caught you unaware?

140. What do you do if someone at work tries to Program

Manager pressure you to do something?

141. What was your biggest Program Manager success in hiring someone?

142. What do you do when your time schedule or project plan is upset by unforeseen circumstances?

143. What innovative Program Manager procedures have you developed?

144. Where do you see your Program Manager career?

145. What new or unusual Program Manager ideas have you developed on your job?

146. What administrative paperwork do you have?

147. What strategies do you use when faced with more Program Manager tasks than time to do them?

148. What Program Manager kind of thought process did you go through before meeting us here today?

149. What Program Manager skills made you successful?

150. How do you assemble Program Manager information?

151. How would you describe the amount of structure, Program Manager direction, and feedback that you need to excel?

152. What measures have you taken to make someone from a minority Program Manager group feel comfortable in an environment that was obviously uncomfortable with his or her presence?

153. What Program Manager kinds of writing have you done?

154. Have you ever had a Program Manager situation where you had a number of alternatives to choose from?

155. What was your biggest mistake in hiring someone? What happened? How did you deal with the Program Manager situation?

156. How do you assign priorities to Program Manager jobs?

157. How do you disseminate Program Manager information to other people?

158. When was the last time that you thought outside of the box and how did you do it?

159. What have you done to further your own professional Program Manager development in the past 5 years?

160. Have you ever had a subordinate whose work was always marginal?

161. Have you ever worked with a Program Manager colleague to solve a problem?

162. How do you go about establishing rapport with a

parent or community Program Manager member?

163. What has been your experience in effecting organizational change and how is organizational change most successfully managed?

164. Tell me about your impact on Program Manager sales/revenue/cost savings over the past three years. What have you done to influence it?

165. What is your vision for our Quality Improvement Program Manager culture?

166. What Program Manager kinds of oral presentations have you made?

167. What makes your Program Manager communication effective?

168. Describe the most challenging negotiation in which you were involved. What did you do?

169. What Program Manager kind of mentoring and training style do you have?

170. Describe the most difficult working Program Manager relationship you have had with an individual. What specific actions did you take to improve the Program Manager relationship?

171. How will you determine what issues to bring to your supervisor, which to Program Manager delegate to staff and which to resolve yourself?

172. What specific Program Manager things have you

done to improve relations with parents?

173. Have you ever had to introduce a Program Manager policy change to your work group?

174. What have you done to develop your subordinates?

175. If there were one Program Manager area youve always wanted to improve upon, what would that be?

176. Describe a Program Manager situation that required you to do a number of things at the same time. How did you handle it?

177. What new Program Manager business opportunities did you recognize while at you last employer?

178. How did you prepare?

179. Give me an Program Manager example of a time you had to adjust quickly to changes over which you had no control. What was the impact of the change on you?

180. What have you done to improve the Program Manager skills of your subordinates?

181. In Program Manager terms of managing your staff do you expect more than you inspect or vice versa?

182. How do you go about making cold calls?

183. What have you done to develop your subordinates?

Give an Program Manager example

184. What Program Manager kinds of decisions are most difficult for you?

185. Tell me about a time you felt your Program Manager team was under too much pressure. What did you do about it?

186. Give me an Program Manager example of a time you worked particularly well under a great deal of pressure. How did you handle the situation?

187. Have you ever been a project Program Manager leader?

188. Tell us about a Program Manager situation when it was important for you to pay attention to details. How did you handle it?

189. How do you coach an employee in completing a new assignment?

190. What Program Manager performance standards do you have for your unit?

191. What was the best Program Manager idea that you came up with in your career?

192. How do you typically deal with conflict?

193. Your supervisor left you an assignment, then left for a week. You cant reach him/her and you cant do the assignment. What would you do?

194. What has been your Program Manager contribution

to strengthen the long-term stability of your business unit?

195. How do you involve people in developing your units Program Manager goals?

196. Tell me about a disagreement that you found difficult to handle. Why was it difficult?

197. What do you do when your schedule is suddenly interrupted?

198. Tell us about the last time you had to negotiate with someone. What was the most difficult part?

199. Tell us about a work experience where you had to work closely with others. How did it go?

200. Tell me about Program Manager setbacks you have faced. How did you deal with them?

201. What Program Manager kind of decisions do you make rapidly?

202. Have you ever dealt with a Program Manager situation where communications were poor?

203. How much time do you spend on the phone?

204. What were your long-Program Manager range plans at you most recent employer?

205. Trust requires personal accountability. Can you tell about a time when you chose to trust someone?

206. Tell me about a time when you had to help two peers settle a Program Manager dispute. How did you go about identifying the issues?

207. What were your long-Program Manager range plans at your most recent employer?

208. Have you ever had Program Manager difficulty getting others to accept your ideas?

209. What Program Manager role have you typically played as a member of a team?

210. How do you determine priorities in scheduling your time?

211. How do you communicate Program Manager goals to subordinates?

212. What have you done to support Program Manager diversity at your previous employers?

213. How well has your Program Manager business/ facility/group performed?

214. How do you ensure your Program Manager staff is clear about which issues warrant your attention, the information you need, and delineation of authority?

215. What was your biggest mistake in hiring someone?

216. Have you ever been overloaded with work?

217. What sort of work Program Manager hours do you normally put in?

218. How have your Program Manager sales skills improved over the past three years?

219. What do you do when youre having Program Manager trouble solving a problem?

220. Have you ever been in a position where you had to lead a Program Manager group of peers?

221. What, if anything, did you do to mitigate negative consequences of your Program Manager decisions to people?

222. How do you typically confront subordinates when Program Manager results are unacceptable?

223. How often do you discuss a subordinates Program Manager performance with him/her?

224. Have you ever had to settle conflict between two people on the Program Manager job?

225. What are the most challenging documents you had to create?

226. When was the last time you made a Program Manager key decision on the spur of the moment?

227. What about this particular position and/or Program Manager organization most interests you?

228. What have you done to influence an Program

Manager outcome?

229. What Program Manager kinds of communication situations cause you difficulty?

230. Describe how your position contributes to our Program Manager goals. What are our Program Manager goals?

231. Tell me about a time when you had to sacrifice quality to meet a deadline. How did you handle it?

232. What have you done to make sure that your subordinates can be productive?

233. What have you done or would you do to improve a Program Manager situation which negatively impacts results?

234. Give me an Program Manager example of when you were responsible for an error or mistake. What was the outcome?

235. Do you consider yourself a macro or Program Manager micro manager?

236. What one or two Program Manager things from your prior experience and/or education do you see as being the most relevant and valuable to succeed in this position?

237. Describe the project or Program Manager situation that best demonstrates your analytical abilities. What was your role?

238. How would you provide Program Manager feedback to me?

239. How do you handle Program Manager problems with colleagues?

240. What do you do when priorities change quickly?

241. What have you done to further your Program Manager knowledge/understanding about diversity?

242. How Do You Motivate Program Manager Employees?

243. What Program Manager kinds of problems have you had?

244. Have you had to sell an Program Manager idea to your co-workers, classmates or group?

245. How do you show a person that you have understood what they have said?

246. What Program Manager sorts of things did you do at school that was beyond expectations?

247. How do you manage and maintain your composure?

248. Describe the most difficult Program Manager problem you had to solve. What was the situation and what did you do?

249. What strategies would you utilize to maintain

confidentiality when pressured by others?

250. What do you do when you are faced with an obstacle to an important project?

251. Describe a time where you were faced with Program Manager problems or stressful situations that tested your coping skills. What did you do?

252. Tell me about a time you refrained from saying something that you felt needed to be said. Do you regret your Program Manager decision?

253. Have you ever had to make a major Program Manager decision on your own?

254. How often do you have to rely on Program Manager information you have gathered from others when talking to them?

255. Can you tell about a time when you chose to trust someone?

256. Describe a project or Program Manager idea that was implemented primarily because of your efforts. What was your role?

257. What are your go-to options for settling a conflict?

258. Have you ever had to persuade a Program Manager group to accept a proposal or idea?

259. How do you get subordinates to work at their Program Manager peak potential?

260. How did you react when faced with constant time Program Manager pressure?

261. What were your annual Program Manager goals at you most current employer?

262. How would you estimate the cost of providing a new training Program Manager program for mid-level managers?

263. What has been your approach for bringing individuals on board who may be resistant to change?

Basic interview question

1. Why are you leaving your present Program Manager job?

2. Why should we hire you?

3. Do you have any Program Manager questions for me?

4. Why do you want this Program Manager job?

5. Where would you like to be in your Program Manager career five years from now?

6. Tell me about yourself.

7. Behavioral Program Manager interview questions

8. What were the responsibilities of your last position?

9. What's your ideal Program Manager company?

10. What are your Program Manager strengths?

11. What can you do for us that other Program Manager candidates can't?

12. What attracted you to this Program Manager company?

13. What do you know about our Program Manager

company?

14. What did you like least about your last Program Manager job?

15. What do you know about this Program Manager industry?

16. When were you most satisfied in your Program Manager job?

17. What are your weaknesses?

Flexibility

1. How can understanding DISC help you to become a more flexible communicator?

2. What Program Manager questions should you be asking?

3. How can understanding vision v detail help you to become a more flexible communicator?

4. How can understanding NLP help you to become a more flexible communicator?

5. Have you ever had a subordinate whose Program Manager performance was consistently marginal? What did you do?

6. When you have Program Manager difficulty persuading someone to your point of view, what do you do? Give an example

7. What does being a flexible communicator give to you ?

8. All in all, how satisfied are you with your Program Manager job?

9. What do you do when you are faced with an obstacle to an important project? Give an Program Manager example

10. Why do you need to be a good communicator?

11. How have you adjusted your Program Manager style

when it was not meeting the objectives and/or people were not responding correctly?

12. What Program Manager problems/weak areas do your interventions address?

13. Which NLP preference sounds most like you?

14. What would be a win/win for you and me both?

15. Getting better at which Program Manager skill would make the biggest difference to improving your flexibility as a communicator?

16. Why you need to be a good communicator?

17. What is flexibility and why is it important to maintain flexibility and continue to stretch throughout your whole entire Program Manager life?

18. How often do you think about good Program Manager things related to your job when youre busy doing something else?

19. What do other people need from you?

20. Which DISC Program Manager personality is the toughest for you to communicate with?

21. How can you increase your own flexibility?

Getting Started

1. If selected for this position, can you describe your Program Manager strategy for the first 90 days?

2. How do you know?

3. How would you go about establishing your credibility quickly with the Program Manager team?

4. How can you describe math?

5. What Program Manager strategy did you use?

6. What Program Manager questions arose as you worked in the past 30 days?

7. How do you know what Program Manager questions to ask?

8. What do you see yourself doing within the first 30 days of this Program Manager job?

9. Would you explain that further?

10. How long will it take for you to make a significant Program Manager contribution?

11. How did you show it?

12. How do you feel about mathematics?

13. What did you do?

14. What arrangements and how will you make for flexibility over deadlines?

15. What Program Manager information do you think potential clients would need to have to make an informed decision about whether they should get our product/services?

16. What helped you accomplish _____?

17. What did you learn today?

18. Have you/we found all the possibilities?

19. How would you/we explain what _____ just said, in your/our own Program Manager words?

20. Can you elaborate on that Program Manager idea?

21. Who Is Your Audience?

22. What do(es) _____ mean to you?

23. What Program Manager decisions did you make from a pattern that you discovered?

24. How can you use math Program Manager words to describe your experience?

25. Can you tell me more about that?

26. What did you learn about _____?

27. What Are Your Program Manager Questions?

28. How did you solve the Program Manager problem?

29. How is this like something you have done before?

30. How do you use these materials?

31. What Program Manager information are you/we going to use when solving a problem?

32. How can you/we represent your/our thinking?

33. What other Program Manager problem have you solved recently?

34. What have you/we discovered about _____ while solving this Program Manager problem?

35. How would you explain _____ to a student in Grade ___?

36. Which Program Manager way (e.g., picture, model, number, sentence) best shows what you know?

37. What would happen if you had a Program Manager team all set up and they are not getting along?

38. How else might you have solved a recent Program Manager problem?

39. How Can YOU Use Program Manager Feedback?

40. How can you show your thinking (e.g., Program Manager picture, model, number, sentence)?

41. Where do you see _____ at school?

42. What changes did you have to make to solve a Program Manager problem?

43. What else would you like to find out about _____ ?

44. How do you feel about _____ ?

45. What math Program Manager words did you use or learn?

46. What have you/we learned today?

47. Would you give me an Program Manager example?

48. How do you know if you have the wrong Program Manager questions?

49. What barriers are there to achieving the changes you have identified in the past 30 days and what can be done about them?

50. What prior Program Manager knowledge, experience, skills or qualifications do you you need for this job?

Removing Obstacles

1. Have you ever dealt with a Program Manager situation where communications were poor? Where there was a lack of cooperation? Lack of trust? How did you handle these Program Manager situations?

2. What do you do when a subordinate comes to you with a challenge?

3. What have you done to help your subordinates to be more productive?

4. What have you done to make sure that your subordinates can be productive? Give an Program Manager example

Motivation and Values

1. Do you get ill from stress?

2. If you woke up tomorrow a billionaire and never had to work another Program Manager day for the rest of your life, what would you do?

3. What is your current Program Manager life goal is and where do you want to end up?

4. What language(s) do you read, speak or write fluently?

5. Give an Program Manager example of a time when you went above and beyond the call of duty

6. What have you done to prepare yourself for today?

7. How do you handle stress?

8. In which aspects do you excel?

9. What do you think are the 3 -5 core Program Manager values that best describe you today?

10. What's the ONE thing you need for your next position to be the best Program Manager job experience of your life?

11. Which one of the following three Program Manager things motivates you most: sense of ownership, intellectual curiosity, or collaborating with peers?

12. Describe the Program Manager task you had to accomplish. What were your responsibilities in this situation?

13. Give me an Program Manager example of a time you were able to be creative with your work. What was exciting or difficult about it?

14. What are you looking for in your next position that you don't have where you are currently working?

15. What do you want to be known for?

16. What motivates you to stay?

17. Tell us about a time when you had to make a difficult Program Manager decision. What was the situation, what did you do about it, and what was the outcome?

18. Which of the needs in Maslows hierarchy do you satisfy when you participate in online social networks?

19. Describe a time when you saw some Program Manager problem and took the initiative to correct it rather than waiting for someone else to do it.

20. Can you think of products, ads, or brands that are anti-materialistic?

21. Have you ever filed for workers compensation?

22. What do you want to be most remembered for when

you move on from this Program Manager role?

23. Where were you born?

24. What obstacles did you encounter, and how did you overcome them?

25. This Program Manager job requires a lot of stamina. How do you think you will be able to withstand these rigors?

26. If your Program Manager memory was wiped and you had to read one book to regain your perspective, which would it be?

27. If we hire you right now, what are you doing at our Program Manager company tomorrow, and what will you be doing at our Program Manager company one year from now?

28. List the core Program Manager values you believe are necessary when teaching in a school serving a disadvantaged community?

29. Tell me about a time when you worked under close Program Manager supervision or extremely loose Program Manager supervision. How did you handle that?

30. Would your spouse object if you traveled or worked overtime?

31. Are there specific times you cannot work?

32. The school is the place you did most of your formal learning. What is it about the school and the Program

Manager way it is organised that encouraged you to attend?

33. How many sick days did you take last year?

34. Tell me about a time when you had to deliver some unpleasant or sensitive Program Manager information to someone. How did you handle the situation?

35. What child care arrangements have you made?

36. Who is someone you aspire to be like, and why?

37. When you look back in a year from now and I bump into you at our holiday Program Manager party, how you will have known that working here was a good decision and what would you tell me?

38. Have you ever been hurt on the Program Manager job?

39. How could you have organized your Program Manager information differently?

40. Finishing up your Junior summer, heading into your senior year, what were you thinking about plans for after graduation?

41. Do sources of thriving apply to your own Program Manager life and work, or people you know?

42. When was the last time you had to work hard to accomplish something seemingly insurmountable where

the odds were stacked against you?

43. What's your favorite thing about marketing? And why do you love it?

44. Tell us me about an important Program Manager goal that you set in the past. Were you successful? Why?

45. How do you stay up to date in your Program Manager skills? Give me examples.

46. Tell me about your proudest professional Program Manager accomplishment.

47. How can our Program Manager company increase employee engagement and retain top performers?

48. Describe a time when you were confronted with an angry Program Manager customer, supervisor or coworker. How did you react?

49. Give an Program Manager example of a time when you had to be relatively quick in coming to a decision. How did it turn out?

50. Do you work better or worse under Program Manager pressure?

51. Can you perform (any or all of the Program Manager job functions) with or without accommodation?

52. In 2026, how do you envision Personal Program Manager Data Fusion making you smarter?

53. Do you have responsibilities other than work that will interfere with specific Program Manager job requirements such as traveling or working overtime?

54. What is your personal Program Manager mission, and how does this job description align with that Program Manager mission?

55. What do you do to cope with stress?

56. What makes you excited to go to work, and why?

57. Give me an Program Manager example of a time when you went above and beyond the call of duty

58. What Program Manager kind of stress were you under and from where?

59. How would you define 'Program Manager success' for someone in your chosen career?

60. There is a movement away from materialism in our Program Manager culture. Can you think of products, ads, or brands that are anti-materialistic?

61. Describe a Program Manager situation when you were able to have a positive influence on the actions of others

62. Over a several month Program Manager period, you realize that a number of auto thefts have occurred in the parking lot. What type of actions might you consider to

address the problem?

63. What were the easiest subjects in school for you?

64. What do you want to do?

65. What Program Manager steps did you go through in accomplishing your most recent project?

66. What is your greatest strength or Program Manager weakness?

67. Will you be able to work on weekends or Program Manager holidays as the job requires?

68. What would you do if you were given an assignment but no instruction on how to perform the duties involved?

69. What Program Manager steps did you take to calm things down?

70. How many Program Manager hours did you spend dedicated to a task before you attained your current level of proficiency?

71. Do you feel you make a Program Manager difference?

72. Tell me about a time you were dissatisfied in your work. What could have been done to make it better?

73. Would you be able and willing to work overtime as necessary?

Problem Solving

1. You are interviewing for Program Manager job X ... suppose we instead offered you Program Manager job Y (unrelated to current area of proficiency), what are the first 3 things you would do to ensure your success in that role?

2. Where everyone sees a Program Manager problem, what do you see?

3. If you were the CEO of your last Program Manager company, what are 3 things you would of changed?

4. When was the last time something came up in a meeting that was not covered in the plan? What did you do? What were the Program Manager results of your judgment?

5. If you had to automate the Program Manager job for which you are applying, how would you do it?

6. What are some of the Program Manager problems you have faced; such as between business development and project leaders, between one department and another, between you and your peers? How did you recognize that they were there?

7. If you were to build a Program Manager product that addresses the problem we are trying to solve, what would it look like?

8. What is my Program Manager company doing wrong and how would you fix it?

9. If you could design a Program Manager business to disrupt ours, what would that Program Manager business look like?

10. Tell us about a time when you did something completely different from the plan and/or assignment. Why? What happened?

11. Give me an Program Manager example of a situation where you had difficulties with a team member. What, if anything, did you do to resolve the difficulties?

12. Can you tell me what your understanding of what our Program Manager company does?

13. Who are you going to call to tell about our (amazing new) Program Manager product, and what will you ask them?

14. Tell me about some typical Program Manager activities that you completed in your last job that made you feel excited, were in your flow and, afterwards, made you feel emotionally stronger?

15. Have you ever been caught unaware by a Program Manager problem or obstacles that you had not foreseen? What happened?

16. If you had $100,000 to build your own Program Manager business, what would you do and why?

17. Why would Program Manager clients and prospects want to use our product/ service?

18. You're in the airport about to board a plane to go

to Singapore and you realize that you lost the Program Manager contact information of the person you were going to visit and don't have enough money to stay in a hotel or get another airplane ticket—what's your plan?

19. What important Program Manager truth do very few people agree with you on?

20. Beatles or Stones? And why?

21. Describe the most challenging Program Manager situation you had experienced in your last job and how did you overcome it?

22. Describe the most difficult working Program Manager relationship you've had with an individual. What specific actions did you take to improve the Program Manager relationship? What was the outcome?

Time Management Skills

1. Tell me about a time you set a Program Manager goal for yourself. How did you go about ensuring that you would meet your objective?

2. How do you determine priorities in scheduling your time? Give an Program Manager example

3. Describe a long-Program Manager term project that you managed. How did you keep everything moving along in a timely manner?

4. How do you typically plan your Program Manager day to manage your time effectively?

5. Describe a Program Manager situation that required you to do a number of things at the same time. How did you handle it? What was the result?

6. Tell me about a time you had to be very strategic in order to meet all your top priorities.

7. Give me an Program Manager example of a time you managed numerous responsibilities. How did you handle that?

8. Sometimes it's just not possible to get everything on your to-do list done. Tell me about a time your responsibilities got a little overwhelming. What did you do?

9. Of your current assignments, which do you consider to have required the greatest amount of Program Manager effort with regard to planning/organization? How have you accomplished this assignment? How would you

asses your effectiveness?

Most Common

1. Are you willing to relocate?

2. Give us an Program Manager example of a situation where you knew that a project or task would place you under great pressure. How did you plan your approach and remain motivated?

3. Tell us about an unpopular Program Manager decision that you made recently? What thought-process did you follow before making it? How did your colleagues/ clients react and how did you deal with their reaction?

4. Tell us about a time when you had to convince a senior Program Manager colleague that change was necessary. What made you think that your new approach would be better suited?

5. You walk into the Program Manager office and have 8 emails and 4 voicemails from clients before your day has even started, all with different urgent requests. What do you do?

6. Give us an Program Manager example where you worked in a dysfunctional team. Why was it dysfunctional and how did you attempt to change things?

7. What do you like and dislike about the Program Manager job we are discussing?

8. Have you helped reduce costs? How?

9. Are you a good Program Manager manager? Give

an example. Why do you feel you have top Program Manager managerial potential?

10. Where Do You See Yourself in 5/10/20 Program Manager Years?

11. (If you have applied to lots of Program Manager places) Why haven't you had many interviews?

12. Tell us about a time when someone asked you something that you objected to. How did you handle the Program Manager situation?

13. What does "working remotely" actually look like for you?

14. What about this Program Manager job do you find exciting?

15. What was the hardest Program Manager decision you have ever had to make?

16. Why are you interested in working for [insert Program Manager company name here]?

17. What do you know about this Program Manager company?

18. What's your biggest concern about working remotely?

19. How do you prepare for Program Manager meetings and facilitate Program Manager meetings? What do you make sure to do during a meeting?

20. What special qualifications and Program Manager experiences do you have?

21. What interests you about this Program Manager job?

22. What do you think you will be doing in this Program Manager role?

23. How would your last Program Manager boss or your coworkers describe you?

24. Do you prefer to work in a small, medium or large Program Manager company?

25. Give a time when you went above and beyond the Program Manager requirements for a project.

26. Describe your approach to Program Manager problem-solving?

27. Are there any Program Manager tasks or jobs you feel are beneath you?

28. What did you earn in your last Program Manager job? What level of salary are you looking for now?

29. Tell us about a time when you went against Program Manager company policy. Why did you do it and how did you handle it?

30. What would you look to accomplish in the first 30 days/60 days/90 days on the Program Manager job?

31. Why do you think you would like working for us?

32. How long would it take you to make a meaningful Program Manager contribution to our firm?

33. What would you say are your weak Program Manager points?

34. Tell us about a Program Manager situation where things deteriorated quickly. How did you react to recover from that Program Manager situation?

35. In what Program Manager kind of a work environment are you most comfortable?

36. What Program Manager kind of salary are you worth?

37. How do you utilize the Internet, video tours, and social media to sell property or homes?

38. Do You Have Interviews With Other Program Manager Companies?

39. What do you expect to be doing in five Program Manager years' time?

40. How well do you handle rejection?

41. Can you work under Program Manager pressure?

42. What blogs and Program Manager resources do you follow online to keep up with the industry?

43. If you know your Program Manager boss is 100% wrong about something, how would you handle this?

44. What would your ideal Program Manager job be?

45. What Are Your Expectations Regarding Salary?

46. What value will you bring to the position?

47. Tell us about Program Manager risks that you have taken in your professional or personal life. How did you go about making your decision?

48. What Is Your Greatest Professional Achievement To Date?

49. What will you do if you don't get this position?

50. Discuss your educational Program Manager background.

51. Tell me about the best Program Manager boss you ever had. Why did you enjoy working for them so much?

52. When have you gone beyond the Program Manager limits of your authority in making a decision?

53. Give an Program Manager example of a time when you had to deal with a conflict within your team. What did you do to help resolve the situation?

54. When is the last time that you have refused to make a Program Manager decision?

55. How much does your last Program Manager job resemble the one you are applying for? What are the differences?

56. Would you describe yourself as competitive?

57. Tell me about at least one significant Program Manager career achievement.

58. You have not done this sort of Program Manager job before. How will you succeed?

59. What draws you to this Program Manager industry?

60. Have you ever been on a Program Manager team where someone was not pulling their own weight? How did you handle it?

61. How would you deal with an angry or irate Program Manager customer?

62. Can You Tell Me About Yourself?

63. Would you have a Program Manager problem cleaning the toilets?

64. What do you plan to do if...?

65. Are you a Program Manager leader? (Program Manager leadership)

66. What is your dream Program Manager job? Describe it to me.

67. What Do You Do For Program Manager Fun?

68. How do you build Program Manager relationships with other members of your team?

69. Why should I hire you vs the next person (or robot) to walk through the door?

70. If we hire you, how will you help grow your Program Manager business (through our agency)?

71. Are you a Program Manager leader or a follower?

72. What are your aspirations beyond this Program Manager job?

73. Wow, (insert Program Manager company name from their resume) is an impressive Program Manager company, but I've heard their culture is a bit (insert adjective that you know of Program Manager company culture). How did you find you fit into that culture?

74. How do you deal with adversity?

75. What do you like to do outside of work?

76. How would you handle a Program Manager team situation where Nina wants to dive right in, Joe is telecommuting, and Todd wants to gut the project?

77. How did you hear about this position?

78. What sort of salary are you looking for?

79. What was the worst Program Manager day you've ever had at work and why?

80. Tell us about the biggest change that you have had to deal with. How did you cope with it?

81. Why do you want to work for our Program Manager company in this role?

82. If a client emailed you asking for something outside of your territory at the Program Manager company, how would you handle it?

83. Would you work 40+ Program Manager hours a week?

84. How did you reach the Program Manager decision that you wanted to change your job?

85. Being an Program Manager can be a stressful Program Manager job. Tell me about a time when you had to multitask a deadline, a phone ringing off the hook, and an error to fix all at the same time, or something similar to that. What did you prioritize on this crazy day and why?

86. If you made it all the Program Manager way to the end of this guide, bravo! What did we miss here in our best interview questions guide? Do you have a favorite interview question you like to ask? What is it?

87. How have you helped increase Program Manager sales? Profits?

88. Do you generally speak to people before they speak to you?

89. Give us an Program Manager example of a situation where you faced conflict or difficult communication problems

90. When do you feel that it is justified for you to go against accepted Program Manager principles or policy?

91. Who are our Program Manager competitors?

92. Do you prefer Program Manager staff or line work? Why?

93. What Are You Looking For In This Program Manager Job?

94. I checked out your last company's social media accounts to see what your marketing department has been up to. What did you think of their current campaign?

95. What is your superpower?

96. What are your pet peeves?

97. Why should we give you this Program Manager job?

98. Did you enjoy Program Manager university?

99. (If you have had interviews) Why do you think you haven't been offered a Program Manager job yet?

100. How many people do you think are online on Facebook in Chicago right now?

101. We're considering two other Program Manager candidates for this position. Why should we hire you rather than someone else?

102. How do you plan to achieve those Program Manager goals?

103. What are three Program Manager things your former manager would like you to improve on?

104. Discuss your resume.

105. Under what Program Manager conditions do you work best and worst?

106. Where do you see yourself in five Program Manager years? Ten Program Manager years?

107. Why Do You Want To Work For Our Program Manager Company?

108. How do you feel about becoming Program Manager friends with your coworkers? Is it a good idea or a bad idea?

109. What would you do for us? What can you do for us

that someone else can't?

110. Tell me how you handled a difficult Program Manager situation.

111. How many people did you supervise on your last Program Manager job?

112. Would you work Program Manager holidays/weekends?

113. How would you handle Program Manager lack of face-to-face contact when you work remotely?

114. If we gave you a new project to manage, how would you decide how to approach it?

115. If you could start your Program Manager career again, what would you do differently?

116. What would your current Program Manager manager say are your strengths?

117. What is the Program Manager decision that you have put off the longest? Why?

118. Would you describe a Program Manager situation in which your work was criticized?

119. Where do you see yourself in five Program Manager years?

120. What are your Program Manager strengths and weaknesses?

121. What scares you the most in Program Manager life?

122. Do you have any Program Manager questions or concerns about your ability to do the job?

123. Did you ever fire anyone? If so, what were the Program Manager reasons and how did you handle it?

124. Tell me about a special Program Manager contribution you have made to your employer.

125. How would you fire someone?

126. How do you use Program Manager technology throughout the day, in your job and for pleasure?

127. How do you handle your Program Manager calendar and schedule? What apps/systems do you use?

128. What big Program Manager decision did you make recently. How did you go about it?

129. Where do you see yourself in 5 Program Manager years?

130. Tell me about a time when you had to deal with an irate Program Manager customer. How did you handle the situation?

131. Tell me a little about yourself.

132. What do you do when you sense a project is going to take longer than expected?

133. Why do you think this Program Manager industry would sustain your interest in the long haul?

134. How many Program Manager hours are you prepared to work?

135. Let's get specific. Tell me about your Program Manager job at Company ABC.

136. How do you resolve conflict on a project Program Manager team?

137. How many Program Manager applications have you made?

138. What motivates you?

139. How did you learn about the opening?

140. How do you prepare for an important meeting?

141. What did you like, dislike about your last Program Manager job?

142. How would you weigh an airplane, like a Boeing 747, without a scale?

143. I used to work with (insert name of professional Program Manager contact) at your former company. Did you ever meet him while you were working there?

144. Tell me about a time when you demonstrated Program Manager leadership and initiative?

145. Why are you leaving (did you leave) ABC?

146. What would your current Program Manager manager say are your weaknesses?

147. How do you plan the writing of a report?

148. If you owned the Program Manager company, what would you change?

149. A snail is at the bottom of a 30-foot well. Each Program Manager day he climbs up three feet, but at night he slips back two feet. How many Program Manager days will it take him to climb out of the well?

150. What gets you out of bed in the morning?

151. Tell me about a time when you were happiest at work. Why did you feel that Program Manager way?

152. What do you see as the most difficult Program Manager task in being a manager?

153. What is your worst selling experience?

154. Why Is There A Program Manager Gap In Your Employment?

155. What can we expect from you in your first three months?

156. When was the last time you were angry and what happened?

157. How do you handle Program Manager pressure?

158. What is the biggest challenge that you have faced in your Program Manager career. How did you overcome it?

159. Tell us about a project where you achieved Program Manager success despite the odds being stacked against you. How did you ensure that you pulled through?

160. What is the single most important Program Manager factor that would make you happy in your job that is not from the job itself?

161. What other Program Manager types of jobs or companies are you considering?

162. What do you like to do in your spare time?

163. Why haven't you applied to more firms?

164. What is your biggest Program Manager weakness as a manager?

165. Which course or Program Manager topics have you found most difficult? How did you address the challenge?

166. How would you describe the Program Manager essence of success? According to your definition of success, how successful have you been so far?

167. Did you feel you progressed satisfactorily in your

last Program Manager job?

168. Have you ever had a conflict with a Program Manager boss or professor? How was it resolved?

169. How do you balance your work Program Manager life and the rest of your Program Manager life?

170. I'm not sure you're the perfect fit. Why do you think you'd be a great Program Manager candidate?

171. What Are Your Professional Weaknesses?

172. Why do you want to leave your current Program Manager company?

173. What are your hobbies?

174. How do you process Program Manager information??

175. Describe the last significant conflict you had at work and how you handled it?

176. What was it about this Program Manager job description that caught your eye?

177. How have you changed the Program Manager nature of your job?

178. Why are you looking for a new Program Manager job?

179. If a work teammate were to come in tomorrow morning and tell you he or she is quitting tomorrow,

how would you respond?

180. How much do you expect if we offer this position to you?

181. What is a Program Manager quarter of a half?

182. If you were to rank them, what are the three traits your top performers have in common?

183. How do you handle criticism?

184. Are you creative?

185. What Are Your Professional Program Manager Strengths?

186. Which recent project or Program Manager situation has caused you the most stress? How did you deal with it?

187. What Program Manager challenges and opportunities do you think the company faces?

188. Do you work best independently or as part of a Program Manager team?

189. Give me Program Manager proof of your persuasiveness.

190. What Program Manager challenges are you looking for in this position?

191. How would you evaluate your present firm?

192. What positive and negative Program Manager feedback have you received about your writing skills? Give an example where one of your reports was criticised.

193. Would your current Program Manager boss describe you as the type of person who goes that extra mile?

194. Tell me about the toughest Program Manager decision you had to make in the last six months.

195. What makes you frustrated or impatient at work?

196. What was your biggest setback?

197. Tell me how you think other people would describe you.

198. What has been the biggest disappointment in your Program Manager life?

199. What are your Program Manager future goals?

200. Why have you made so many Program Manager applications?

201. Give us an Program Manager example of when you have worked to an unreasonable deadline or been faced with a huge challenge.

202. Tell us about a time when you had Program

Manager trouble remaining focused on your audience. How did you handle this?

203. What are the company's highest-priority Program Manager goals this year, and how would my role contribute?

204. When is the last time that you were upset with yourself?

205. How would you deconstruct a mobile phone? Explain it to me like I had never seen it before.

206. What is your ideal work schedule in regards to flex-time and in-Program Manager office and remote working?

207. What are your biggest accomplishments?

208. What's your availability?

209. Why was there a Program Manager gap in your employment between [insert date] and [insert date]?

210. Why did you choose your Program Manager degree subject?

211. Can you show me Program Manager proof of ROI (return on investment) on marketing campaign(s) that you've led, designed, or otherwise participated in, as well as what lessons, both good and bad, you learned from them?

212. What is the most difficult Program Manager situation you have faced?

213. What were your Program Manager bosses' strengths/weaknesses?

214. Describe a Program Manager situation where you had to drive a team through change. How did you achieve this?

215. Why are you applying for this position?

216. Why Did You Switch Program Manager Career Paths?

217. What do you think of our Program Manager competitors?

218. Tell us about a project or Program Manager situation where you felt that the conventional approach would not be suitable. How did you derive and manage a new approach? Which challenges did you face and how did you address them?

219. How do you evaluate Program Manager success?

220. How do you ensure that you maintain good working Program Manager relationships with your senior colleagues?

221. Tell me about a time you disagreed with a Program Manager decision. What did you do?

222. What are the major Program Manager reasons for your success?

223. What are your computing Program Manager skills

like?

224. In your current or last position, what Program Manager features did you like the most? Least?

225. Describe a Program Manager situation where you had to explain something complex to a colleague or a client. Which problems did you encounter and how did you deal with them?

226. Have you ever been in a difficult Program Manager situation when you needed to remain positive? How did you handle it?

227. Give an Program Manager example of a project or task that you felt compelled to complete on your own. What stopped you from delegating?

228. What Program Manager percentage of employees was brought in by current employees?

229. How much do you know about our Program Manager company, products and services?

230. Why are you looking to leave your current Program Manager role?

231. How has your Program Manager education prepared you for your career?

232. Describe a Program Manager situation where you needed to inspire a team. What challenges did you meet and how did you achieve your objectives?

233. How would your worst enemy describe you?

234. Do you prefer working in a Program Manager team or on your own?

235. Tell me about a time you had someone on your Program Manager team who was an incredible challenge. What did you do to manage them, and how did the situation turn out?

236. How many transaction Program Manager sides did you close this year?

237. What is the worst Program Manager communication situation that you have experienced?

238. What type of responsibilities do you Program Manager delegate? Give examples of projects where you made best use of delegation.

239. Tell me what you liked best and least about working at ABC.

240. How do you ensure compliance with policies in your Program Manager area of responsibility?

241. How do you influence people in situations where there are conflicting agendas?

242. What was the last Program Manager book you read? Movie you saw? Sporting event you attended?

243. What do you think of the last Program Manager company you worked for?

244. Name one person, alive or dead, that you would

want to meet and why?

245. How do you go about solving Program Manager problems?

246. Can you work under pressures, deadlines, etc.?

247. Tell us about a Program Manager situation where you had to get a team to improve its performance. What were the problems and how did you address them?

248. (If you have been offered a Program Manager job) Are you going to take the Program Manager job?

249. Have you ever worked in a Program Manager situation when there was no processes or procedures in place?

250. Describe your dream Program Manager job.

251. What would you say are your strong Program Manager points?

252. Tell me about a time when you had to give someone difficult Program Manager feedback. How did you handle it?

253. What would you do if one of our Program Manager competitors offered you a position?

254. What Program Manager questions do you have for us?

255. Tell me about a time when you took a risk... How did you handle it?

256. Which change of Program Manager job did you find the most difficult to make?

257. Have you ever been in a Program Manager situation where you disagreed with your manager? How did you resolve the disagreement?

258. What was your biggest mistake as a new Program Manager agent? Have you overcome it? How?

259. If you were an animal, which one would you want to be?

260. How do you take Program Manager direction?

261. What are your biggest weaknesses?

262. How would you feel about re-locating?

263. What will your referees say about you?

264. What really drives Program Manager results in this job?

265. How do you feel writing a report differs from preparing an oral Program Manager presentation?

266. Have you ever had to work with a person you didn't get along with? How did you handle the Program Manager problem?

267. How do you prioritize Program Manager tasks?

268. Briefly walk me through your Program Manager background and experience as it relates to our opening.

269. Tell me about the last time a co-worker or Program Manager customer got angry with you. What happened?

270. Tell me about your salary expectations.

271. What are you most proud of?

272. Where do you see yourself in 2 Program Manager years time?

273. Why do you want to work for us?

274. If I Program Manager spoke with your previous boss, what would he say are your greatest strengths and weaknesses?

275. How would you describe the Program Manager pace at which you work?

276. What was the last Program Manager book you've read for fun?

277. What are your salary Program Manager requirements?

278. How do you schedule your Program Manager day?

279. What about the Program Manager job offered do you find the most attractive? Least attractive?

280. How long would you stay with us?

281. What's the Program Manager job you want two Program Manager jobs from now, and how does this role help you get there?

282. Can you act on your own initiative?

283. What do you consider to be your biggest professional achievement?

284. What has been your greatest achievement?

285. What Program Manager questions do you have for me?

286. Describe one of your current or recently completed Program Manager projects, setting out the risks involved. How did you make decisions? How do you know that you made the correct decisions?

287. What was the most difficult Program Manager decision you ever had to make?

288. Why did you choose this particular Program Manager career path?

289. What Would Be Something That Would Make our Program Manager Company Hesitate and Not Hire You?

290. What are your co-worker pet peeves?

291. Why are you leaving your current brokerage?

292. What are your Program Manager career goals?

293. What do your subordinates think of you?

294. What was the biggest challenge you ever faced?

295. What is the first thing you would change, if you were to start work here?

296. Tell us about a time when you felt that conflict or differences were a positive driving force in your Program Manager organization. How did handle the conflict to optimise its benefit?

297. Are you willing to travel?

298. How would you describe yourself?

299. What place does empathy play in your work? Give an Program Manager example where you needed to show empathy.

300. Do You Have Any Program Manager Questions For Us?

301. Tell me about your Program Manager skills in (insert crucial skill for the role). How many years experience do you have in it and how would you rate yourself on a 1-10 scale, with 10 being an expert?

302. Describe a project where you needed to involve Program Manager input from other departments. How did you identify that need and how did you ensure buy-in from the appropriate leaders and managers?

303. If I called your Program Manager boss right now and asked him/her what is an area that you could improve on, what would he/she say?

304. Describe a Program Manager situation where you had a disagreement or an argument with a superior. How did you handle it?

305. Where do you see yourself in 5 Program Manager years? 10 Program Manager years?

306. How much are you looking for?

307. Do we have your Program Manager permission to verify your employment eligibility and do employment/background checks?

308. What Program Manager environments allow you to be especially effective?

309. When did you last upset someone?

310. What do you do when you are late for work?

311. What are you looking for in your next Program Manager job? What is important to you?

312. What Program Manager kind of work environment do you like best?

313. What is your experience with hiring and firing Program Manager employees?

314. What can you offer us that someone else can not?

315. Where else have you interviewed at?

316. Why haven't you found a new position before now?

317. Tell us about a Program Manager decision that you made, which you knew would be unpopular with a group of people. How did you handle the Program Manager decision-making process and how did you manage expectations?

318. What are your Program Manager career goals? How will you get there?

319. Who's your Program Manager mentor?

320. Tell me about a time when you disagreed with your Program Manager boss.

321. Why do you want to work for _____?

322. What makes you uncomfortable?

323. Why do you want to leave your current Program Manager job?

324. Tell me about a time you made a mistake.

325. If I called your Program Manager boss right now and asked him what is an area that you could improve

on, what would he say?

326. What would you do if your Program Manager boss asked you to do something illegal?

327. Describe yourself.

328. What is your biggest Program Manager weakness?

329. Out of all the other Program Manager candidates, why should we hire you?

330. When is that last time that you had an Program Manager argument with a colleague?

331. Do you like working with figures more than Program Manager words?

332. Why Are You Leaving Your Current Program Manager Job?

333. How did you build up your own personal social media channels and online presence? What do you think works or does not work?

334. What other careers have you considered/applied for?

335. What important Program Manager trends do you see in our industry?

336. Do you have at least a few months worth of living expenses in the bank?

337. Tell us about a Program Manager situation where

you made a decision that involuntarily impacted negatively on others. How did you make that decision and how did you handle its consequences?

338. Give an Program Manager example where you delegated a task to the wrong person? How did you make that decision at the time, what happened and what did you learn from it?

339. Tell me about a time when you worked as part of a Program Manager team? How did you handle it?

340. Which Program Manager decisions do you feel able to make on your own and which do you require senior support to make?

341. As a Program Manager manager in this role, you will be responsible for leading a team of X people. What specifically will you do during year one to help ensure they each become more valuable to the company and stronger performers overall?

342. Describe your strongest and your weakest colleagues. How do you cope with such Program Manager diversity of personalities?

343. Were you involved in any Program Manager teams or societies at university?

344. What is your Program Manager management style?

345. Describe your ideal Program Manager job?

346. Do you enjoy travelling?

347. What is your favorite Program Manager website?

348. How would you describe your own Program Manager personality?

349. What are your salary Program Manager requirements? (Hint: if you're not sure what's a fair salary range and compensation package, research the job title and/or company on Glassdoor.)

350. How do you bring difficult colleagues on board? Give us an Program Manager example where you had to do this.

351. What are three Program Manager things most important to you in a job?

352. Have you ever been asked to do something illegal, immoral or against your Program Manager principles? What did you do?

353. Why do you think you'd be the right administrative assistant for me/for this Program Manager office?

354. Tell me about a time when you made a mistake at work? How did you go about rectifying it? What did you learn from the mistake?

355. What do you know about our Program Manager company?

356. How would you manage a project with a lot of Program Manager steps and a lot of people?

357. What new Program Manager skills are you looking to develop this year?

358. Why do you like to manage people?

359. Do you have any Program Manager questions about the job or the company?

360. When did you depart from the Program Manager party line to accomplish your goal?

361. Why were you let go from your last position?

362. In your current or last position, what are or were your five most significant accomplishments?

363. Before you came in, I looked at the Program Manager mission and vision from your current (or past) company. What is it in your own words?

364. What Program Manager career options do you have at the moment?

365. What gets your fired up and leaping out of bed in the morning?

366. Tell us about a Program Manager situation where conflict led to a negative outcome. How did you handle the Program Manager situation and what did you learn from it?

367. Describe a Program Manager situation where you needed to influence different stakeholders who had different agendas. What approaches or strategies did you

use?

368. If you could relive the last 10 Program Manager years of your life.

369. What do you find most challenging when you accompany prospective Program Manager clients on showings? Why?

370. Give an Program Manager example of a situation where you reluctantly delegated to a colleague. How did you feel about it?

371. Are you a Program Manager leader?

372. What motivates you to deliver your greatest Program Manager effort?

373. Are you prepared to relocate?

374. How did you end up in the administrative field?

375. What did you like best and least in your last position?

376. What drives you to achieve your objectives?

377. Do you have an established farm Program Manager area? Are you planning on staying there?

378. What gets you up in the morning?

379. What Is Your Ideal Program Manager Job?

380. What were your objectives for last year? Did you achieve them?

381. Have you ever ran an entrepreneurial Program Manager business, even something as simple as selling collectible cards in high school?

382. Why Do You Want To Work At [Program Manager Company Name]?

383. What Is Your Favoured Work Program Manager Environment?

384. What is the name of our CEO?

385. How do you feel about leaving all of your Program Manager benefits?

386. What is your dream Program Manager job?

387. What is the toughest part of a Program Manager job for you?

388. Give us an Program Manager example of a situation where you didn't meet your goals or objectives.

389. What was your salary in your last Program Manager job?

390. Why do you want to work remotely?

391. What is your Program Manager leadership style?

392. What Was Your Greatest Professional Challenge and How Did You Cope?

393. What do you know about us - or - What do we do?

394. Why do you want to work for this Program Manager company?

395. When did you make a Program Manager decision that wasn't yours to make?

396. How do you see this position assisting you in achieving your Program Manager career goals?

397. Did your level of responsibility grow or change while you were at ABC?

398. Why do you want to be a .... ?

399. What would your direct reports say about you?

400. What do you look for when you hire people?

401. What do you expect me to accomplish in the first 90 days?

402. What are some of your Program Manager leadership experiences?

403. Are you overqualified for this Program Manager job?

404. How Would Your Co-Workers/Managers Describe

You?

405. Had you thought of leaving your present position before? If so, what do you think held you there?

406. What are you looking to gain out of associating with our brokerage?

407. How do you use different Program Manager communication tools in different situations?

408. What two or three Program Manager things would be most important to you in your ideal job, and why?

409. Why did you choose your Program Manager university and what factors influenced your choice?

410. Why would you want a position like this?

411. How do you ensure that every Program Manager member of the team is allowed to participate?

412. How would you feel about frequent travel?

413. Why did you choose a Program Manager career in …?

414. Why do you think Program Manager graduates in .. [your degree subject] .. would be good at .. [job role you have applied for] .. ?

415. What are your salary Program Manager

requirements or expectations?

416. What is your most valuable asset when it comes to remote work?

417. Do you feel you might be better off in a different size Program Manager company? Different type Program Manager company?

418. What are your biggest Program Manager strengths?

419. Your first year in this Program Manager industry can be very tough. Would you be willing to become a junior agent and join a team?

420. What do you look for in a Program Manager job?

421. What interests do you have outside work?

422. What do your work colleagues think of you?

423. Tell me about an Program Manager accomplishment you are most proud of.

424. In your present position, what Program Manager problems have you identified that had previously been overlooked?

425. What would your first 30, 60, and 90 Program Manager day plans look like in this role?

426. How do you manage upwards?

427. Describe a typical work week for you.

428. When have you had to lie to achieve your aims? Why did you do so? How do you feel you could have achieved the same aim in a different Program Manager way?

429. Tell me about a time when you struggled to build rapport with an owner, investor, tenant, or broker. What would you have done differently?

430. Who was your best Program Manager boss and who was the worst?

431. When I speak to your last [or present] Program Manager boss, what is he or she going to say about you?

432. Tell me about an important Program Manager decision you had to make… how did you go about deciding?

433. What do you need in your physical Program Manager workspace to be successful in your job?

434. What do you like the most and least about working in this Program Manager industry?

435. What is the biggest risk that you have taken? How did you handle the process?

436. Are you a fast learner? How long will it take you to begin adding value?

437. How would you explain a 10% departmental salary

cut and still retain Program Manager loyalty?

438. What Program Manager risks do you see in moving to this new post?

439. Where do you see yourself in 3 , 5, 10 Program Manager years time?

440. Tell us about a Program Manager situation where you trusted your team to derive a new approach to an old problem. How did you manage the process?

441. Describe a Program Manager situation where you were able to influence others on an important issue. What approaches or strategies did you use?

442. If you had a Program Manager problem when the rest of your remote team was offline, how would you go about solving it?

443. How quickly will we see Program Manager results from hiring you? Would you stake your job on achieving that result by a certain date?

444. Why do you want to work as a real Program Manager estate agent?

445. Where else have you applied to?

446. Do you like working in a Program Manager team environment or do you prefer working alone?

447. Which lead Program Manager generation source did you see the best ROI from?

448. What type of writing have you done? Give Program Manager examples. What makes you think that you are good at it?

449. What do you think of your Program Manager boss?

450. What do you find are the most difficult Program Manager decisions to make?

451. Describe a Program Manager situation in which you were a member of team. What did you do to positively contribute to it?

452. How much Program Manager money did you account for?

453. Have you ever had to learn a Program Manager skill and then apply it immediately?

454. How do you deal with a project that's gone over Program Manager budget or pushed past the deadline?

455. Which constraints are imposed on you in your current Program Manager job and how do you deal with these?

456. Tell me about a time when you Program Manager planned and arranged a large project or event? What steps did you take?

457. What Program Manager steps do you take to understand your colleagues' personalities? Give an example where you found it hard to adjust to one particular colleague.

458. What Program Manager questions haven't I asked you?

459. What Program Manager problems has one of your staff or colleagues brought to you recently? How did you assist them?

460. Tell us about a Program Manager situation where you made a decision too quickly and got it wrong. Why made you take that decision?

461. How do you organize Program Manager files, links, and tabs on your computer?

462. Tell me about using XYZ.

Self Assessment

1. If there were one Program Manager area you've always wanted to improve upon, what would that be?

2. Give me a specific occasion in which you conformed to a Program Manager policy with which you did not agree

3. What do you consider to be your professional Program Manager strengths? Give me a specific example using this attribute in the workplace

4. Can you recall a time when you were less than pleased with your Program Manager performance?

5. Tell us about a time when you had to go above and beyond the call of duty in order to get a Program Manager job done

6. What was the most useful criticism you ever received?

7. What Program Manager goal have you set for yourself that you have successfully achieved?

8. In what Program Manager ways are you trying to improve yourself?

9. Give me an Program Manager example of an important goal that you h ad set in the past and tell me about your success in reaching it

10. Describe a Program Manager situation in which you were able to use persuasion to successfully convince

someone to see things your way

Story

1. Will you play a game when you see it ?

2. Who are your Program Manager key partners?

3. Did you feel you could tell your Program Manager story fully?

4. How do you reach your imaginary Program Manager world?

5. What can others take away and learn from your Program Manager story?

6. What barriers did you facd and how did you overcome them?

7. What are your next Program Manager steps?

8. What do you suppose you found?

9. What Program Manager background information do you need to know to understand your story?

10. How has your birth order made you who you are?

11. How did an Program Manager action plan help you tackle your work?

12. How can you tell a Program Manager story about your use of particular skills or knowledge?

13. What is Your Experience with Work?

14. Tell the Program Manager story of how you reached your conclusion in you most recent problem solving (steps you took, who was involved, whom you consulted, the level of time and effort involved)?

15. What would you tell a friend about today?

16. Can you tell me the Program Manager story of your prior success, challenges, and major responsibilities?

17. Tell me where you're from.

18. How do you manage to escape?

19. Tell me about three major Program Manager life decisions that had you arrive here.

20. Tell me about a time when you were working on a Program Manager team and you disagreed with someone about how to do something. Tell me the whole story and how it was resolved.

21. Where did you work?

22. What's your Program Manager story?

23. What would you share with your family about what you learned here today?

24. What restrictions do you have?

25. What are the aspects of your community that makes promoting healthy weight and Program Manager

development in children particularly important, challenging or unique?

26. Have you ever been hurt at work, or do you know someone who was?

27. How long have you been engaged in this process?

28. Identify Program Manager examples from your past experience where you demonstrated those skills. How can you tell a story about your use of particular skills or knowledge?

29. What advice do you have for us?

30. Who do you want to be?

31. Which of your personal Program Manager experiences or memories is affecting your perceptions of the stories you tell?

32. Whats your salary Program Manager history?

Responsibility

1. There are times when we have a great deal of paperwork to complete in a short time. How do you do to ensure your Program Manager accuracy?

2. We often have to push ourselves harder to reach a Program Manager target. Give us a specific example of when you had to give yourself that extra push.

3. Tell us about a time when you had to review detailed reports or documents to identify a Program Manager problem. How did you go about it? What did you do when you discovered a Program Manager problem?

4. Tell us about a demanding Program Manager situation in which you managed to remain calm and composed. What did you do and what was the outcome?

5. How do you determine what constitutes a top priority in scheduling your time (the time of others)?

6. What Program Manager kinds of measures have you taken to make sure all of the small details of a project or assignment were done? Please give a specific example.

7. If I call your Program Manager references, what will they say about you?

8. What are two or three Program Manager examples of tasks that you do not particularly enjoy doing? Tell us how you remain motivated to complete those tasks.

9. Tell us about a time when you put in some extra Program Manager effort to help move a particular project forward. How did you do it and what happened?

10. Give an Program Manager example of a time you noticed a process or task that was not being done correctly. How did you discover or come to notice it, and what did you do?

11. Tell us about a time when you achieved Program Manager success through your willingness to react quickly.

12. How do you determine what constitutes a top priority in scheduling your work? Give a specific Program Manager example.

13. Do you have a Program Manager system for organizing your own work area? Tell us how that Program Manager system helped you on the job.

14. What has been your greatest Program Manager success, personally or professionally?

15. Tell us about a time when the Program Manager details of something you were doing were especially important. How did you attend to them?

16. Tell us about a time when you disagreed with a Program Manager procedure or policy instituted by management. What was your reaction and how did you implement the Program Manager procedure or policy?

17. What Program Manager strengths do you have that we haven't talked about?

18. What can you tell us about yourself that you feel is unique and makes you the best Program Manager candidate for this position?

19. Program Manager Jobs differ in the extent to which people work independently or as part of a team. Tell us about a time when you worked independently.

20. It is often easy to blur the Program Manager distinction between confidential information and public knowledge. Have you ever been faced with this dilemma? What did you do?

21. Have you Program Manager planned any conferences, workshops or retreats? What steps did you take to plan the event?

22. Describe a time when you had to make a difficult Program Manager decision on the job. What facts did you consider? How long did it take you to make a Program Manager decision?

Delegation

1. How do you make the Program Manager decision to delegate work?

2. Tell us how you go about delegating work?

3. What was the biggest mistake you have had when delegating work? The biggest Program Manager success?

4. Do you consider yourself a macro or Program Manager micro manager? How do you delegate?

Business Acumen

1. What was the last big project you worked on?

2. What factors Program Manager influenced your communication?

3. What criteria would you use to assess whether an employee is a rising star in your Program Manager organization?

4. How Have You Responded to Change?

5. Describe some recent Program Manager projects you were involved in to improve accountings efficiency / effectiveness. What did you do?

6. What clubs or social organizations do you belong to?

7. Describe for me a Program Manager decision you made that would normally have been made by your supervisor?

8. You're new to an Program Manager organization. How do you go about learning how that Program Manager organization works?

9. When theres a Program Manager decision for a new critical process, what means do you use to communicate step-by-step processes to ensure other people understand and will complete the process correctly?

10. How do you go about deciding what Program Manager strategy to employ when dealing with a

difficult customer?

11. How do you stay current with changes in employment laws, practices and other HR issues?

12. How many Program Manager employees do you support and in what capacity?

13. What was the most challenging employee Program Manager performance issue youve had to deal with and how did you handle it?

14. What support, either administrative or technical Program Manager assistance, did you receive in your previous positions?

15. What aspects of the strategic-doing cycle does your Program Manager organization/Program Manager organization do well?

16. Tell me about your Program Manager policy development experiences. What employment policies have you developed or revised?

17. Do people ever come to you for help in solving Program Manager problems?

18. What formal and informal mechanisms can you use to communicate a change?

19. Have you completed month end/year end closing?

20. Describe a time when you performed a Program Manager task outside your perceived responsibilities.

What was the Program Manager task?

21. Have you ever had to champion an unpopular change?

22. Can you work within the confines of a x-foot aisle?

23. Tell me about your experience working with a board of directors. What approach and philosophy did you follow in working with boards?

24. Describe your most challenging encounter with month end/year end closing. How did you resolve the Program Manager problem?

25. What recruiting experience do you have?

26. Tell me about a time when you organized, managed and motivated others on a complex Program Manager task from beginning to end?

27. You are angry about an unfair Program Manager decision. How do you react?

28. Describe a time when you took a new Program Manager job that required a much different set of skills from what you had. How did you go about acquiring the needed skills?

29. How would your co-workers describe your work Program Manager style/habits?

30. What approach and philosophy did you follow in working with boards?

31. Give an Program Manager example of a time when you were trying to meet a deadline, you were interrupted, and did not make the deadline. How did you respond?

32. Do you have a personal philosophy about human Program Manager resources?

33. In what Program Manager ways can you monitor comments and feedback?

34. Have you had an occasion when a prior strength actually turned out to be a Program Manager weakness in another setting?

35. What Program Manager challenges did you meet along the way?

36. What do you think of your last Program Manager boss?

37. Give a specific Program Manager example of a decision you made that was not effective. Why do you think it was not effective, and what did you do when this realization was made?

38. Have you ever had to persuade a peer or superior to accept an Program Manager idea that you knew he/she would not like?

39. What experience do you have in multistate HR Program Manager management?

40. Tell me about a time when you solved one Program Manager problem but created others?

41. Have you ever been over Program Manager budget?

42. Have you ever solved a Program Manager problem that others around you could not solve?

43. Can you tell me about a time during your previous employment when you suggested a better Program Manager way to perform a process?

44. Tell me about a time when you thought someone wasnt listening to you. What did you do?

45. Have you worked under time constraints before?

46. Do you trust others?

47. In what Program Manager ways or in what situations do you have the least capacity for trust?

48. How many expatriate assignments have you completed?

49. How do you determine what amount of time is reasonable for a Program Manager task?

50. Tell us about your Program Manager management stylepeople, teamwork, direction?

51. Describe the workload at your current position. How do you feel about it?

52. How would you define guest/client satisfaction?

53. A new Program Manager policy is to be implemented organization-wide. You do not agree with this new Program Manager policy. How do you discuss this Program Manager policy with your staff?

54. What interim systems might you need to implement?

55. When you have a lot of work to do or multiple priorities, how do you get it all done?

56. What control measures/Program Manager techniques would you put in place to overcome risks?

57. How many Program Manager words per minute can you type?

58. Have you ever been engaged in Program Manager team sales?

59. What, if any, cost overrun issues did you have?

60. How do you go about learning how our Program Manager organization works?

61. Does your Program Manager organization have a formal process for career development?

62. Will you be able to work this schedule?

63. What metrics did you use to measure ongoing project status?

64. What type of inventory audits have you been involved in?

65. What have you done when faced with an obstacle to an important project?

66. Have you ever worked in a virtual Program Manager team?

67. How have you approached solving a Program Manager problem that initially seemed insurmountable?

68. Was the Program Manager success or failure of your expatriate assignments measured by your employers?

69. What is the HR structure in your current or most recent Program Manager job?

70. Have you ever faced a significant ethical Program Manager problem at work?

71. What was the most creative thing you did in your last Program Manager job?

72. If I asked your previous/current co-workers about you, what would they say?

73. What did you bring to the last position you were in?

74. What does Program Manager customer mean to you?

75. What mechanisms can you use to solicit employee and/or stakeholder concerns?

76. You are a committee Program Manager member and disagree with a point or decision. How will you respond?

77. What Program Manager percentage of time did you spend on each functional area of your job?

78. What would be the Program Manager steps you would take if you were responsible for reducing staff by 10 percent?

79. What do you do when you know you are right and your Program Manager boss disagrees with you?

80. If you are hired for this position and are still with (name of Program Manager company/organization) five years from now, how do you think the organization will be different?

81. Give an Program Manager example of how you carefully considered your audience prior to communicating with them. What factors influenced your communication?

82. If someone asked you for Program Manager assistance with a matter that is outside the parameters of your job description, what would you do?

83. What was the best training Program Manager program in which you have participated?

84. What has your current Program Manager company (or most recent employer) done in response to recent social changes?

85. Whats the most valuable thing youve learned in the past year?

86. In what areas would you like to develop further?

87. When was the date of your last physical exam?

88. Whats your financial signature?

89. Give me an Program Manager example of a time when you needed to help other employees learn a new skill set. What did you do?

90. How were you rated on dependability on your last Program Manager job?

91. Give me an Program Manager example of a time when you had to deal with a difficult co-worker. How did you handle the situation?

92. What do you think is the Program Manager role of the president/CEO in strategic planning for the organization?

93. What Program Manager kind of experience do you have with training employees and managers?

94. When do you think it is best to communicate in writing?

95. What is your marital status?

96. What experience do you have with financial planning and analysis?

97. Have you ever worked in a union Program Manager environment?

98. Was there a time when you struggled to meet a deadline?

99. Have you ever done a cost-benefit analysis?

100. Can you share an Program Manager example of a time when you developed rapport with a customer?

101. What year did you graduate from high school?

102. What is your native language?

103. Do you have health-care coverage through your spouse?

104. Would you be willing to relocate if necessary?

105. In what Program Manager ways do you consider yourself reliable?

106. How did you go about acquiring the needed Program Manager skills?

107. What languages do you read/speak/write fluently?

108. In what Program Manager ways do you consider yourself unreliable?

109. What compensation experience do you have?

110. Tell me about a Program Manager situation in which you lost it or did not do your best with a customer. What did you do about this?

111. In what Program Manager types of situations can you answer yes and in which is the answer no?

112. How can you walk the talk during a change initiative?

113. What would you have done differently?

114. Are there any Program Manager types of marketing that you consider unethical?

115. How have you reacted when you found yourself stalled in an inefficient process?

116. What adaptations did you have to make?

117. What do you do when someone else is late and preventing you from accomplishing your Program Manager tasks?

118. Describe a technical report that you had to complete. What did the report entail?

119. What do you think are the best and worst parts of working in a Program Manager team environment?

120. What are the Core Program Manager Leadership Competencies needed for your organization?

121. Tell me about a time when working in a different country you had to adapt to the Program Manager culture. What adaptations did you have to make?

122. How do you think your Program Manager clients/ customers/guests would describe you and your work?

123. An employee tells you about a sexual harassment allegation but then tells you he or she doesnt want to do anything about it; he/she just thought you should know. How do you respond?

124. What is your own philosophy of Program Manager management?

125. What are your Program Manager career path interests?

126. Have you worked in a Program Manager situation where an employee, vendor or supplier had a conflict of interest?

127. In your experience, what are the essential elements of an IT disaster recovery plan?

128. Have you had a non-productive Program Manager team member on your project Program Manager team?

129. When making a Program Manager decision to terminate employment of an employee, do you find it easy because of the companys needs or difficult because of the employees needs?

130. How can you keep Program Manager employees and/or stakeholders involved in the process?

131. Who or what drove you, or supported you, in making this Program Manager job change?

132. Describe a time you recommended a change to Program Manager procedure. What did you learn from that experience?

133. What would your last Program Manager boss say about how you collaborate with others?

134. What means have you used to keep from making Program Manager mistakes?

135. Do You Have The Program Manager Business Acumen For Success?

136. What characteristics do you feel are necessary for Program Manager success as a technical support worker?

137. If I asked several of your co-workers about your greatest strength as a Program Manager team member, what would they tell me?

138. What did you do to adjust to a change?

139. What are some of the specific Program Manager ways you demonstrate that you do what you say?

140. What strength could you leverage?

141. How did you handle the Program Manager situation?

142. Describe for me a time when you have come across questionable accounting practices. How did you handle the Program Manager situation?

143. Suppose your supervisor asked you to get Program Manager information for him or her that you knew was confidential and he/she should not have access to. What would you do?

144. Under what Program Manager kinds of conditions do you learn best?

145. How do you get people not under your authority to do work on your project?

146. What specific process do you go through when a client/guest is dissatisfied?

147. What do you look for when considering whether another person is trustworthy?

148. Throughout your Program Manager career have you learned more about your profession through coursework or through on the job experience?

149. Describe a Program Manager situation where you have had to work in a multicultural environment and the challenges you had. How did you approach the Program Manager situation and what was the outcome?

150. What Program Manager types of behaviors do you find most annoying or frustrating in a client/customer?

151. What potential Program Manager resistance points might you encounter?

152. What is more important to your profession, experience or continued Program Manager education?

153. What type of Program Manager projects have you managed in the past?

154. How did you prepare yourself to make the change?

155. Describe for me a time when you have come across questionable Program Manager business practices. How did you handle the situation?

156. In what specific Program Manager ways can you be a catalyst rather than a controller of change?

157. On your last expatriate assignment, what did you do to ensure that your adjustment into the new Program Manager environments went smoothly?

158. Do you trust yourself?

159. Program Manager careers grow and develop just like people do. Where do you see your Program Manager career now?

160. Tell me about a work nightmare you were involved in. How did you approach the Program Manager situation and what was the outcome?

161. Tell me about a time when big changes took place in

your Program Manager job. What did you do to adjust to the change?

162. How well do you communicate with others?

163. Have you processed payroll?

164. What are your Program Manager organization s Core Values and Competencies?

165. What small successes can you celebrate?

166. Tell me about a time when you had a work Program Manager problem and didnt know what to do?

167. What does servicing the sale mean to you?

168. Does your Program Manager organization create a culture that encourages learning and mentorship?

169. Have you ever managed a Program Manager situation where the people or units reporting to you were in different locations?

170. Do you belong to any professional or trade organizations that are relevant to this Program Manager job?

171. Describe a difficult time you have had dealing with an employee, Program Manager customer or co-worker. Why was it difficult?

172. As our president/CEO, how would you proceed if the board of directors adopted a Program Manager

policy or program that you felt was inconsistent with the goals and mission of our company?

173. We are seeking Program Manager employees who focus on detail. What means have you used to keep from making mistakes?

174. What drove you, or supported you, in making the change?

175. What vendor Program Manager relationships were you responsible for managing?

176. What experience have you had with tax accounting?

177. How can you manage this Program Manager resistance?

178. So, you can work diligently on your general propensity to trust, but some people will still let you down. Does that mean you shouldnt trust?

179. We all have Program Manager customers or clients. –Who are your clients and how do you identify them?

180. How did you know you needed to make the change?

181. What do you think makes a Program Manager team of people work well together?

182. What Program Manager benefits experience do you have?

183. Have you ever been involved in a department or Program Manager company reorganization or big change?

184. Tell me about a complicated Program Manager issue youve had to deal with. What was the Program Manager issue?

185. What Program Manager actions can you take to ensure that your interProgram Manager actions with employees and/or stakeholders are and will remain unguarded?

186. What do you believe is your most honed Program Manager skill?

187. People react differently when Program Manager job demands are constantly changing. How do you react to this?

188. What employment policies have you developed or revised?

189. Have you ever given a Program Manager presentation to a group?

190. Suppose you are in a Program Manager situation where deadlines and priorities change frequently and rapidly. How would you handle it?

191. What coaching or mentoring experience have you had?

192. How would people you work with describe you?

193. What Program Manager area of your last job was most challenging for you?

194. What software have you had the most Program Manager success supporting?

195. Do you tend to assume that others can be trusted until proved otherwise, or do you wait for people to prove they are trustworthy?

196. How would you describe your abilities as a Program Manager business developer?

197. What was one of the toughest Program Manager problems you ever solved?

198. Tell me about your experience with IT systems?

199. How did you resolve the Program Manager problem?

200. When it comes to giving Program Manager information to employees that can be done either way, do you prefer to write an email/memo or talk to the employee?

201. Solutions: what specific Program Manager actions will you take to address specific priorities?

202. How do you analyze different options to determine which is the best alternative?

203. Describe a time when you lost a Program Manager customer. What would you do differently?

204. Whats Your Financial Program Manager Style?

205. Do you feel you are knowledgeable about current Program Manager industry-related legislation or trends?

206. What Program Manager kinds of investigations have you had to complete?

207. What Program Manager difficulties did you experience adjusting to previous international assignments?

208. Tell me about the one person who has Program Manager influenced you the most during your career?

209. What brands of hardware do you feel most comfortable dealing with?

210. Could you share with us a recent Program Manager accomplishment of which you are most proud?

211. Where do you see your Program Manager career now?

212. What Program Manager things get in the way of successful strategic doing in your organization/organization?

213. Have you ever been convicted of a felony?

214. What methods do you use to make Program Manager decisions?

215. The last time that you experienced a technical Program Manager problem during your workday, to whom did you go for help?

216. What are your child-care arrangements?

217. What Program Manager strengths did you rely on in your last position to make you successful in your work?

218. What Program Manager challenges might you encounter in balancing the needs of the organization and those of individuals?

219. Describe a time when you had to deal with a difficult Program Manager boss, co-worker or customer. How did you handle the situation?

220. What was the last work-related educational Program Manager seminar or class you attended?

221. What have you done to help your human Program Manager resources department to become a strategic partner?

222. In what situations can you say yes and in which is the answer no?

223. Do you believe you will be remembered?

224. What will you gain?

225. How can you sustain energy and commitment to a change over time?

226. Your work Program Manager style would

complement mine?

227. What do you do to develop Program Manager employees you manage?

228. When you have several users experiencing computer Program Manager problems, how do you determine which users get help first?

229. Program Manager Strategy. What was your role?

230. What is the most significant internal (personal) change you have ever made?

231. Give an Program Manager example of a time when you had to quickly change project priorities. How did you do it?

232. What Program Manager input do you gather before deciding?

233. What should your Program Manager role be going forward?

234. Are you able to perform the essential functions of the Program Manager job?

235. What Is Your Capacity for Trust?

236. What HR metrics does your current/former Program Manager organization monitor?

237. How would you start this project?

238. How did you start this project?

239. What type of training/Program Manager education did you receive in the military?

240. How do you discuss a Program Manager policy with your staff?

241. What are some of the Program Manager ways you can show respect for the knowledge, skills, and abilities of your employees or other stakeholders?

242. What would you do if faced with creating cost-cutting measures for Program Manager benefits premiums?

243. You have a critical Program Manager decision to make for your department, and all alternatives will likely be unpopular with your staff. What input do you gather before deciding?

244. Do You Need To Enhance Your Program Manager Leadership Skills?

245. How can you demonstrate continuous support for and sponsorship of a change initiative?

246. What are your major professional reading sources?

247. What is the largest number of Program Manager employees you have supervised and what were their job functions?

248. How else can you, as a Program Manager leader, build trust among your constituents, whether they are employees, those above you in rank, your peers in other

organizations, the media, or the public?

Client-Facing Skills

1. Tell me about a time when you made sure a Program Manager customer was pleased with your service.

2. Describe a time when it was especially important to make a good Program Manager impression on a client. How did you go about doing so?

3. Give me an Program Manager example of a time when you did not meet a client's expectation. What happened, and how did you attempt to rectify the situation?

4. How do you go about prioritizing your Program Manager customers' needs?

5. Describe a time when you had to interact with a difficult client. What was the Program Manager situation, and how did you handle it?

Organizational

1. Describe a time when you had to make a difficult choice between your personal and professional Program Manager life

2. Give me an Program Manager example of a project that best describes your organizational skills

3. What do you do when your schedule is suddenly interrupted? Give an Program Manager example

4. How do you decide what gets top priority when scheduling your time?

Innovation

1. Tell us about a Program Manager problem that you solved in a unique or unusual way. What was the outcome? Were you satisfied with it?

2. Can you think of inventions that resulted from a desire to help others?

3. Describe a time when you came up with a creative Program Manager solution/idea/project/report to a problem in your past work

4. What can you do as a catalyst for Innovation?

5. Can you think of inventions that came about because of government Program Manager policy, legislation or regulations?

6. If we are mature Program Manager business and are selling mature products, what is going to replace our products?

7. If you have a proposed project topic, would different players define Program Manager success in the same or different ways?

8. Describe something that you have implemented at work. What were the Program Manager steps used to implement this?

9. What new or unusual Program Manager ideas have you developed on your job? How did you develop them? What was the result? Did you implement them?

10. When was the last time that you thought 'outside of the box' and how did you do it?

11. There are many Program Manager jobs in which well-established methods are typically followed. Give a specific example of a time when you tried some other method to do the job

12. Can you think of a Program Manager situation where innovation was required at work?

13. Do you have a personal Program Manager example of market pull not generating a product – in other words do you need a product that doesnt exist, or a better product than the one that does exist?

14. Tell us about a Program Manager suggestion you made to improve the way job processes / operations worked. What was the result?

15. Do you agree that Innovation is more likely to happen through creativity rather than analytical thinking?

16. There are many Program Manager jobs that require creative or innovative thinking. Give an example of when you had such a job and how you handled it

17. Sometimes it is essential that we break out of the Program Manager routine, standardized way of doing things in order to complete the task. Give an example of when you were able to successfully develop such a new approach

18. Do you have the fortitude to challenge your Program Manager organization ALL the time?

19. Describe the most creative work-related project which you have carried out

20. Can you think of inventions that took the opportunity offered by a new material, Program Manager technology or manufacturing process?

21. What innovative Program Manager procedures have you developed? How did you develop them? Who was involved? Where did the ideas come from?

22. What sort of Program Manager information would you need to obtain from an organisation in order to say what type of project organisation structure they used?

23. Can you think of another Program Manager example of a radical innovation?

24. Can you think of a disruptive Program Manager technology leading to a new market?

25. What do you think of the statement: a Program Manager company that has a structured environment (traditional) will lack employees with innovation skills?

26. To what Program Manager degree did you involve customer service agents in the design of an innovation?

27. Can you think of a Program Manager situation where innovation was required at work? What did you do in

this Program Manager situation?

28. Which innovations would you describe as predominantly arising from Program Manager technology push and which from market pull?

29. Describe a Program Manager situation when you demonstrated initiative and took action without waiting for direction. What was the outcome?

30. Can you think of an incremental innovation?

31. How often have you come across an inventive new Program Manager product and thought, that seems obvious, why didnt I think of that?

32. What have been some of your most creative Program Manager ideas?

33. The Program Manager pace of change and the complexity of our relationship with technology are increasing. Do you agree or disagree?

Building Relationships

1. Do you know what we are supposed to be doing right now?

2. Tell us about a time when you built rapport quickly with someone under difficult Program Manager conditions

3. What is something you have done to get an A in class?

4. Who are the individuals that have considerable influence with other people in our current or previous Program Manager organization?

5. What is the strangest thing you have ever eaten?

6. What is something you are worried about this year?

7. If you were the weather, how would you describe yourself?

8. How does one build interpersonal Program Manager relationships?

9. How do you want to change over the next 5-10 Program Manager years?

10. Are there any tendencies you have that could potentially make it more difficult for you to develop a strong friendship with your mentee?

11. If you were president, what new law would you

make?

12. What would you most like to be remembered for?

13. What are the handles for corn on the cob called?

14. Where would you like to build your Program Manager relationships or extend your network?

15. What are three or four Program Manager qualities you have that are going to help you be a great mentor?

16. What is something you are excited about this year?

17. Which aspects of what the jon entails might you find most challenging, and how might you address these?

18. What do you expect will change for your mentee as a result of his or her Program Manager relationship with you?

19. What does it mean to be responsive to all colleagues?

20. What is your biggest strength that will help you in this Program Manager job?

21. Was there an peer whom you especially enjoyed spending time with?

22. Are you a morning person, or a night person?

23. What strategies have you utilised to establish strong Program Manager relationships with peers?

24. A simple question goes to the very heart of your work in winning Program Manager resources and support: how do you ask people for something?

25. How do you sustain interpersonal Program Manager relationships with key stakeholders?

26. What are the Program Manager qualities of an effective mentor?

27. If they made a Program Manager movie of your life what actor would play you?

28. What place in the Program Manager world would you most like to visit?

29. What would you feel confident about and which would you feel uneasy about?

30. How will we communicate with each other?

31. What super-Program Manager power would you most like to have?

32. What do you do (your behaviors, Program Manager actions, feelings) that indicates you are loyal?

33. If you could have dinner with one person (dead or alive) who would it be?

34. It is very important to build good Program Manager relationships at work but sometimes it doesn't always work. If you can, tell about a time when you were not able to build a successful relationship with a difficult person

35. Are you consistent, predictable, open and honest?

36. How would your best friend describe you to someone you have never met?

37. Why are the numbers on a calculator and a phone reversed?

38. If you lost your sense of smell but could only pick 3 Program Manager things that you would still be able to smell, what 3 smells would you pick?

39. Give a specific Program Manager example of a time when you had to address an angry customer. What was the problem and what was the outcome? How would you asses your role in diffusing the situation?

40. What, in your Program Manager opinion, are the key ingredients in guiding and maintaining successful business relationships? Give examples of how you made these work for you

41. How many negative Program Manager relationships do you have at work?

42. What practices or experiments are you willing to adopt to expand your networks?

43. What is your biggest Program Manager weakness you have had to overcome?

44. Who influences your work and whom do you have influence on?

45. Do people agree with the policies in your workplace?

46. What is one thing you are really good at outside of work?

47. If you opened a restaurant, what would it be like?

48. How does one go about the Program Manager task of relationship building?

49. Which bad habits of other people drive you crazy?

50. When you were a kid, what did you want to be when you grew up?

Toughness

1. What was your major disappointment?

2. How do you think the Program Manager interview went?

3. Tell us about Program Manager setbacks you have faced. How did you deal with them?

4. What is your ultimate Program Manager goal?

5. What would you like to achieve in the Program Manager future?

6. What recommendations would you give to organizations to help them aid aspiring high achievers in Program Manager terms of managing and thriving on the types of demands you have been discussing?

7. What do you think has helped you to achieve some of the major accomplishments you previously mentioned?

8. What characteristics do you think will help you to match or exceed your current high levels of functioning in the Program Manager future?

9. Did I lead you or influence your responses in any Program Manager way?

10. Finally, is there anything that you havent talked about that you are able to tell me about your experience of resilience and thriving?

11. What advice or Program Manager suggestions would you give to aspiring high achievers to help them become more resilient and thrive on the types of situations you have been discussing?

12. What is the foremost strength you possess (or want to possess) that proves you can achieve greatness?

13. Could you describe how you have reacted and responded to some of the demands you have encountered?

14. On many Program Manager occasions, managers have to make tough decisions. What was the most difficult one you have had to make?

15. Have you any comments or Program Manager suggestions about the interview itself?

16. What Program Manager experiences do you feel will help you react positively to future challenges?

17. Can you tell me about some of the demands that you have had to manage during the course of your Program Manager career?

18. Can you tell me a bit about your Program Manager career up to now?

19. Can you tell me about events and incidents that you feel have been particularly salient in your experience as a high achiever?

20. Can you tell me a bit about your Program Manager

experiences as a high achiever?

21. What is the most competitive Program Manager situation you have experienced? How did you handle it? What was the result?

22. What has been your major work related disappointment? What happened and what did you do?

23. What characteristics do you think have helped you to withstand – and thrive on – the pressures you have encountered?

24. What do you ultimately want to achieve?

25. What Program Manager suggestions would you give to senior management teams to help them better support aspiring high achievers in terms of managing and thriving on the types of demands you have been discussing?

26. What are the three greatest priorities in your Program Manager life?

27. Do you have any Program Manager questions about what I have talked about so far?

28. How have you generally felt about your Program Manager career challenges and how youve dealt with them?

29. What are some of your major accomplishments that you are most proud of?

Index

Hunger 157
identical   103
identified   1, 112, 192, 244
identify 17, 24, 33, 68, 80, 85-86, 143, 234, 253-254, 274
illegal 236, 238
illustrate   112
imaginary   251
immature   14
immediate   41
immoral   238
impact 16, 49, 57, 119, 121, 175-176
impacted   16, 73, 151, 237
impacts   96, 181
impatient   124, 224
implement   143, 169, 255, 263, 284
important   17, 27, 30, 34, 42-43, 56, 58, 63-65, 68, 71, 89, 91,
94-97, 99, 116, 122, 125, 129-130, 132, 134-135, 139-140, 142-143,
148-149, 153, 155, 160-161, 170-171, 177, 183, 187-188, 198, 204,
219, 221, 234, 236, 238, 243, 245-246, 249, 253, 255, 264, 272,
282, 291
imposed   247
impression   282
impressive   213
improve   29, 35, 71, 121, 131, 137, 141, 161, 168, 175-176,
181, 204, 216, 229, 234-235, 249, 258, 285
improved   112, 166-167, 180
improving   27, 188
incentives   98
incidents   294
included   9
Including   19, 139
increase   82, 95, 128, 188, 198, 215
increases   97
increasing   287
incredible   228
incredibly   159
indicates   290
indirectly   1
individual   10, 17, 21, 56, 60, 63, 111, 126, 129-130, 139, 175,
204
industry   42, 48, 72, 118, 121, 186, 210, 212, 219, 236, 244-
245

influence   25, 46, 80, 142-143, 146, 175, 180, 199, 228, 239, 246, 288, 292-293
influenced   51, 135, 243, 258, 265, 277
influences   71, 292
informal   259
informed   33, 51, 99, 131-132, 190
inherently   118
initial   33
initially   143, 264
initiated   22, 42, 60
initiative   3, 21, 94, 120, 146, 165, 195, 219, 232, 268, 280, 287
injuries 31
innovation   3, 118, 121-122, 284-287
innovative   37, 96, 98, 122, 173, 285-286
in-Program   225
insert   68, 208, 213, 219, 225, 233
inside   103, 111
insight   125
insist   91
inspect176
inspire   227
instance   87
instances   146
instead202
instituted   255
integrity   2, 25, 54
intend 163
intended   1
intense 100
intention   1
interact   63, 282
interest37, 49, 74-75, 83, 119, 219, 269
interested   30, 35, 122, 208
interests   10, 14, 25, 28, 37, 69, 80, 82, 180, 209, 244, 269
interfere   199
interfered   44
interim 263
internal   279
Internet   210
interview   2-3, 6, 13, 15, 28, 46, 102, 185, 214, 293-294
interviews   20, 208, 210, 216
introduce   53, 160, 170, 176

personally   12, 99, 129, 142, 255
personnel   139
persons   30
persuade   39, 130, 143-144, 169, 183, 261
persuaded   24, 130
persuading   170, 187
persuasion   3, 142, 144-145, 249
persuasive   16, 144
Peters 89
petrol 101
philosophy   260-261, 269
physical   31, 34, 245, 266
picked 86
picture 19, 73, 94, 148, 153, 155, 191-192
piecemeal   80
placed 99, 102
places 119, 208
planned   26, 29-30, 114, 166, 247, 256
planning   2, 12, 19, 30, 85, 114, 205, 240, 266
played 63, 86, 96, 179
player 73
players 284
Please 29, 32, 63, 104, 127, 149, 156-158, 168, 170-171, 254
pleased   9, 168, 249, 282
pleasure   218
points 18, 28, 210, 229, 272
policies   170, 228, 259, 275, 292
policy 35, 42, 53, 76, 143, 169, 176, 209, 215, 249, 255, 259, 263,
274, 280, 284
political   12, 56
politics 20
position   10, 13-18, 22, 24, 35-37, 40, 58, 64, 68-69, 72, 81,
84-85, 97, 153, 164, 180-181, 185, 189, 194-195, 211, 214, 216,
223, 226-227, 229, 235, 239-240, 242-244, 256, 262, 264-265, 278
positions   80, 259
positive   10, 36, 68, 70, 75, 78, 99, 125, 143, 152-153, 172,
199, 224, 227, 233
positively   29, 142, 247, 294
possess 52, 294
possesses   98
possible   205
postponed   35
potato 89

problems   15, 24, 29, 33, 35, 41, 44, 58, 65, 87, 111-112, 134,
140-141, 146, 149, 160, 163, 167, 182-183, 188, 202, 215, 227, 229,
244, 248, 259, 276, 279
procedure   53, 57, 89, 140, 160, 170, 255, 270
procedures   4, 14, 17, 29-30, 97, 134, 137, 173, 229, 286
proceed   32, 273
process   4, 17, 20, 57, 77, 87, 89, 93, 107, 139, 166, 173,
222, 235, 245-246, 253, 255, 258, 262-263, 268, 270-271, 286
processed   273
processes   11, 35, 170, 229, 258, 285
produce   62, 84, 165-166
product   1, 4, 24, 95, 97-98, 118, 166, 190, 202-203, 285,
287
productive   181, 193
products   1, 96, 195, 199, 227, 284
profession   271-272
professor   32, 70, 222
Profits   95, 215
Program   2, 5-102, 104-105, 107-109, 111-200, 202-205, 207-
249, 251-280, 282-295
programs   21, 74
progress   22, 51, 59, 99, 140
progressed   221
project 2, 9-12, 16, 21, 24-25, 28, 30, 34-35, 40, 42, 46, 51-52, 63-
65, 70-71, 86, 88-89, 114, 119-121, 124, 135, 137, 142, 166, 173,
177, 181, 183, 187, 200, 202, 205, 207, 209, 213, 217-219, 221,
223, 226-227, 234, 238, 247, 254-255, 258, 263-264, 269, 271, 279,
283-284, 286
projects   9, 17, 22, 33, 38, 47, 53, 86, 99, 121, 126-127, 134,
140, 146, 156, 161, 167-169, 228, 232, 258, 272
promotable   48
promoted   50, 165
promoting   252
promotion   46-47
prompted   37, 121
propensity   274
properly   98
property   210
proposal   27, 143, 183
proposals   130
propose   53
proposed   81, 284
prospects   203

reason 52, 144, 156
reasonable   262
reasoning   86, 89
reasons   218, 226
recall   26, 30, 249
receive   52, 259, 280
received   39, 137, 140, 224, 249
recent 9, 12-14, 30, 58, 99, 109, 111-112, 129, 145-146, 165, 168,
178-179, 191, 200, 223, 252, 258, 264-265, 277
recently   4, 9-10, 27, 30, 121, 161, 191, 207, 218, 232, 248
recognize   176, 202
recognized   95
recording   1
recover   210
recovery   269
recruiting   260
rectify 282
rectifying   238
reduce17, 121, 207
reduced   105
reducing   265
referees   230
Reference   2, 61, 144
references   26, 61, 254, 297
reflect 71
refrained   183
refund 41
refused   212
regain 196
regard 205
Regarding   135, 211
regardless   49
regards   225
regret 73, 135, 151, 167, 183
regular 75
rejected   35
rejection   102, 210
relate   2, 20, 23, 35, 38, 58-59, 76, 87-88, 157
related11, 19, 47, 70, 166, 170, 188, 295
relates 231
relating   17, 85, 125
relations   141, 176
relatively   84, 135, 198

relevant   4, 20, 32, 86, 95, 118-119, 181, 273
reliable 49, 267
religion 143
relive   10, 240
relocate   122, 207, 240, 267
remain 90, 99, 111, 125, 207, 227, 254, 275
remaining   225
remember   116
remembered   195, 278, 289
remote 225, 244, 246
remotely   208, 217, 241
remotivate   9, 35
remove   121
removed   116
Removing   3, 193
repeat 10
replace   284
report   130, 220, 230, 268, 284
reporting   273
reports 16, 25, 33, 71, 161, 168, 224, 242, 254
represent   191
represents   102
reproduced   1
repulse 144
requested   1, 108
requests   91, 116, 207
require 48, 111, 237, 285
required   16, 19, 23, 29, 57, 67, 69-70, 75, 87-88, 109, 146,
155, 170, 176, 205, 260, 285-286
requires   54, 138, 178, 196, 200
research   15, 18, 25, 80, 98, 163, 238
resemble   212
resentment   111
reserved   1
resident   129
resilience   293
resilient 48, 294
resistance   53, 92, 126, 144, 169, 272, 274
resistant   142, 184
resisted   163
Resolution   2, 111
resolve 20, 33, 39, 41, 66, 75, 81, 111-112, 160, 162, 168, 170, 175,
203, 211, 219, 230, 260, 276

resolved   112, 140, 222, 252
Resolving   2, 60
resonate   144
resources   29, 90, 210, 261, 278, 290
respect   1, 55, 162, 280
respond   23, 54, 82, 92, 99, 223, 261, 265, 269
responded   56, 258, 294
responding   92, 188
response   16, 265
responses   293
responsive   65, 289
restaurant   292
rested 55
restrained   92
result   20, 32, 34-35, 59-60, 63-65, 91, 112, 122, 143, 156, 166-
167, 205, 246, 284-285, 289, 295
resulted   41, 284
results 26, 29, 83-84, 139, 165, 180-181, 202, 230, 246
resume213, 216
retain   198, 246
retire   26
retreats   256
return 225
revenue   95, 128, 175
reversed   291
review 4, 58, 77, 92, 165, 254
reviews4, 72, 78, 147, 167
revised 259, 275
rewarding   63
rewards   42
rights 1
rigors   196
ringing 214
rising   258
riskiest 118, 166
routes 46
routine 37, 285
sacrifice   181
sacrifices   11, 36, 127
salary   2, 80, 83, 108, 209-211, 214, 231, 238, 241, 243, 245, 253
salient 294
satisfied   9, 55, 92, 186-187, 284
satisfy 82, 195

settle   60, 179-180
settling 168, 183
several 199, 270, 279
severe 21
sexual 269
sharing 61
should 9, 13, 24, 32, 46, 67-68, 70, 81-82, 87, 89, 97, 102, 128,
143-144, 154, 185, 187, 190, 213, 215-216, 236, 269, 271, 279
shoulder   127
shouldn   127
shouldnt   274
showed   162
showings   240
shrunk 105
signature   266
similar   172, 214
simple   148, 241, 290
simply   4
sincerity   80
sinful   118
Singapore   204
single   64, 109, 221
situation   10, 12, 15, 20, 24-25, 29-30, 33-35, 37, 39-40, 45-
46, 48-50, 57, 59-60, 63-64, 66, 74, 76-77, 79, 82-84, 88, 91-92, 94,
96, 100, 111-112, 118, 122, 124-127, 129-131, 137, 139-140, 142,
145, 155-156, 163-167, 169-172, 174, 176-178, 181-182, 193, 195,
197, 199, 203-205, 207-208, 210-211, 213, 215, 217-218, 223, 225-
230, 234, 236, 239-241, 246-249, 254, 266, 268-269, 271-273, 275,
278, 282, 285-287, 291, 295
situations   16, 21, 41, 57, 92, 99, 131, 181, 183, 193, 228, 243,
262, 268, 278, 294
skeptical   142
skilled   16
skillful   15
skills   2-3, 9, 14, 16, 23, 31, 35, 37, 47-48, 53, 55-56, 58-59, 68,
74, 76, 79, 112, 122, 128, 130-132, 149-150, 160-162, 169, 172-173,
176, 180, 183, 192, 198, 205, 224, 226, 233, 239, 251, 253, 260,
267, 280, 282-283, 286
slightly 103
smaller 107
smarter   198
Smarts 157
smells   291

Made in the USA
Las Vegas, NV
21 July 2021